The

Pocket Book
of
Animals

The
Pocket Book
of
Animals

John Mitchinson
John Lloyd

Designed and illustrated by Ted Dewan

faber and faber

First published in 2007
by Faber and Faber Ltd
Bloomsbury House
74–77 Great Russell Street
London WC1B 3DA

This pocket edition first published 2009

Typeset by Ted Dewan and Palindrome
Printed in England by CPI BookMarque, Croydon

Consultant Editor
Christopher Gray

Researchers
James Harkin
Mat Coward
Jenny Doughty
Molly Oldfield
Justin Gayner

A CIP record for this book
is available from the British Library

ISBN 978–0–571–24513–0

2 4 6 8 10 9 7 5 3 1

Contents

Foreword

Stephen Fry

Animals are the oats in the QI muesli, the basic black frock in our wardrobe, the baseline to our phat phunky dub. If you cannot be entranced, amused and astonished by the animal kingdom then QI has no use for you nor you, no doubt, for us.

Animals have this in common with each other: unlike humans they appear to spend every minute of every hour of every day of their lives being themselves. A tree frog (so far as we can ascertain) doesn't wake up in the morning feeling guilty that it was a bad tree-frog the night before, nor does it spend any time wishing it were a wallaby or a crane-fly. It just gets on with the business of being a tree-frog, a job it does supremely well. We humans, well . . . we are never content, always guilty, and rarely that good at being what nature asked us to be – *Homo sapiens*.

There is much to be learned from the animals. Much to be learned about them, of course, but much, much more to be learned about ourselves: our limits, our lonely uniqueness as a species and, I would add, our greatness. The fact that we care with unreciprocated fervour about woodlice, woodpeckers and wolverines is to our credit. I cannot subscribe to this modern idea that we should feel guilty about our role on earth, or inferior for having evolved a (self-)conscious mind. This is just

Genesis wrapped up in new, even more sanctimonious clothes. The old religion and the new orthodoxy both claim we have guardianship over the earth and a 'moral' responsibility for its destiny. Well, fine. But I will not apologise for committing the crime of being born any more than a marmot or a mosquito should. And between them, those two have been responsible for more death and upheaval than all human wars.

In the end, whatever weird and unfathomable purposes there might be to existence, to whichever theory of the development of life you might subscribe, we all have to face the fact that there is no entirely satisfactory explanation for the oddities and extremities of the zoological world. Nothing in nature seems to follow a fixed predictable law, not the number of penises on an insect, not the need for a chicken to have a head. I suppose they all have in common the melancholy fact that they have been impersonated, with the use of nothing more than a mop of hair, expressive hands and a pair of big brown eyes, by Mr Alan Davies.

Forepaw

Alan Davies

My ignorance of animals is legendary.

I know two dogs quite well. One is my dad's the other is my step-mum's. Both these dogs are idiots. I know my sister's cat quite well as she is actually my cat but I gave her to my sister to look after for a fortnight in 1993. I have two goldfish, one named Brian after Brian Dowling out of TV's *Big Brother* and the other named Bill after Bill Bailey, the legendary materialist-hippy comedian from the West Country who has many animals of different kinds. Bill gave me Bill to keep in my pond when he was having the builders in to move his pond 20 feet up the garden (money well spent). Bill and Brian (the fish) get on very well. Bill and Brian the television personalities have, to the best of my knowledge, never met. I can only speculate on how their relationship would unfold. Amicably at first but I suspect they may baulk at being asked to spend five years together in a 6-foot x 6-foot pond as their fishy counterparts have. I don't know what sex the fish are but even if they are opposites they will not be able to have babies because the moment they lay any eggs they will eat them. In the wild they forget where they've put them, so the tiny Nemos have a fighting chance. In captivity they will inevitably come across them and simply forget they have laid and fertilised them. This is not because they were drunk at the time but because goldfish have a famously short memory. Or is that a modern myth the QI folk would publicly shame me for believing? Probably. My ignorance of animals is only extended by a refusal to eat them. Although I did eat meat throughout my childhood and remember lamb in particular as being bloody delicious. Jeremy Clarkson turned to me during a recording of QI one night and said pityingly: 'You're a vegetablist aren't you?' QI's creator and senior boffin, John Lloyd, on learning that I would eat a prawn but on no account a mammal, simply shook his head and whispered, 'Extraordinary.' I don't know why I won't eat them, it just seems so unnecessary. Fish I do eat because they were here long before we were and they'll be here long after we've gone. No, that's not it. It's because they are cold-blooded and don't have a nervous system like mammals so they don't feel pain. Who knows if that's true? Selfishly, I eat seafood because it's hard to get decent veggie food in restaurants. Except Indian restaurants. Or Thai. Or Vietnamese. That's why those Asian cuisines really float my boat. Delicious food and nothing died.

Unfortunately, of course, in many parts of Asia, they do eat dogs. And I like dogs even though both the dogs I know are idiots . . .

Introduction

John Mitchinson & John Lloyd

Animals know things we don't. You may think this is pretty obvious, but in a book about 'animal ignorance' it's important to point out who it is that's ignorant here. Spend a little time in the company of animals, even the ones stretched out on the bottom of your bed, and you'll start to see the world differently. Look into their eyes and try to think what they're thinking. It's impossible, of course, which is what makes it so compelling. Whatever else we discover, however close we come to understanding the inner workings of the universe, we'll never, ever know what it feels like to live life as a cat, still less an ant, or a starfish.

Animals have fired our imaginations like nothing else, not God, not the weather, not other humans. From the first moment we discovered we could daub shapes on cave walls, we've been painting, writing and thinking about them. The magical rituals of hunter-gatherer peoples, their creations myths and healing practices are all one long dialogue with the animal kingdom. To take on the power of an animal – the sight of an eagle, the speed of an antelope, the strength of a lion – these were the original superpowers. Most animals are still tirelessly exercising the same skills they've done for millennia. As a species, we're very new kids on a very old block.

The original inspiration for this book was the medieval bestiaries. These were the most popular and influential books after the Bible itself. In them you'd be amazed to discover that weasels conceived through their ears, that bees were born from dead oxen and that a goat's blood was hot enough to dissolve diamonds. And scattered among the myths about real animals was 'real' information about mythical beasts – centaurs, unicorns, dragons, manticores. Only rarely did bestiaries contain facts based on actual observation of nature. But nobody seemed to mind, the stories were too good to miss and anyway the real point was to teach human beings how to behave. What we liked was the idea of a collection of animals that didn't leave you disappointed, as zoos so often do: a modern bestiary, based on zoological fact. After all, European eels swimming back and forth to Bermuda, octopuses' arms that crawl for a month after they've been severed, mites so small they live inside a bee's throat, or eight-legged water bears that can stay in a state of suspended animation for a century – these are even more outlandish than the wildest fantasies of the bestiary writers. They just happen to be true.

So, here are a hundred animals, some supposedly familiar, some definitely obscure, all of them, without exception, quite interesting. We might easily have called it *The Book of Animal Engineering*. Ted Dewan trained as an engineer and, as his brilliant drawings show, how animals work is almost as mind-altering as how they behave. But this is not a workshop manual. Nor is it a reference book, or an animal rights polemic; it's a menagerie, an armchair safari. It teaches only one unambiguous truth: that the word 'natural' is meaningless. Animal strategies for feeding, reproducing or just getting about are so madly various, so utterly, gloriously perverse that you end up believing that absolutely anything is possible.

And that's the point. Animals cheer us up. They don't need us to patronise them, or to speak for them. But after studying them in such detail, it's impossible not to feel they deserve our respect. The great American naturalist Henry Beston once wrote: 'In a world older and more complete than ours, they move finished and complete, gifted with the extension of the senses we have lost or never attained, living by voices we shall never hear. They are not brethren, they are not underlings: they are other nations, caught with ourselves in the net of life and time.'

So come down to the waterhole of ignorance and wallow with us for a while.

The missing link between animals
and the real human being
is most likely
ourselves.

KONRAD LORENZ
Austrian zoologist and animal psychologist

Aardvark
Ancient, odd and out on its own

Aardvarks are the last survivors of a primitive group of mammals that have lived in Africa since the dinosaurs. They were originally classified alongside anteaters and armadillos in the order *Edentata* ('no teeth'), but they are not remotely related, having evolved on different land masses.

In fact, aardvarks don't have any close relatives: they are the only mammal species that boasts an entire order to itself. *Tubulidentata* means 'tube-toothed' and aardvark teeth are completely different from those of any other animal. They are twenty flat-topped pegs, made up of hexagonal tubes, right at the back of their mouths. Instead of enamel, they are are covered with *cementum*, the stuff that is normally inside teeth. Like rodents' teeth, they never stop growing.

The aardvark has a primitive 'designed by committee' look to it: the nose of an anteater, the ears of a donkey, the feet of a rabbit and the tail of a giant rat. But don't be fooled: it has outlasted many other species because it does one thing supremely well. It is a termite-eating machine.

As soon as darkness falls it leaves its burrow and applies its snout to the ground, snuffling

Aardvarks are loners: it's rare for them to meet up except to mate

in huge zigzags across the savannah in search of mounds to crack open and lick clean. It can cover 30 miles and hoover up over 10 pints of termites in a single evening. The aardvark nose contains more bones and scent receptors than that of any other mammal. Its ears can pick up the tiniest of underground movements and its powerful claws tear open mounds that would blunt a pickaxe. Aardvarks are strong: they can grow to the size of a rugby forward and dig a burrow faster than six men using shovels.

Their thick skin protects them from termite bites and as the long, sticky tongue reels in supper, they can close their nostrils at will, to stop the insects running up inside.

They have also built up a remarkably beneficial relationship with a plant known as the 'aardvark cucumber' that grows its fruits underground. Aardvarks dig them up and eat them when water is scarce, then bury their seed-laden droppings, ensuring the plants' survival. The *San* (bushmen) of the Kalahari call the fruit 'aardvark dung'.

Humans and hyenas are the only predators that will attack a fighting fit aardvark. Despite its solitary, reclusive nature, a cornered aardvark is a formidable foe, slashing with its claws, kicking its legs, and executing high-speed forward somersaults.

TERMITE TAKE-AWAY

Once they've opened a termite mound, aardvarks will eat up to 500,000 termites in a sitting

Aardvarks are hunted for meat and leather: *aardvark* is Afrikaans for 'earth pig' and they are said to taste like gamey pork. They are also called 'ant bears' but their Latin name, *Orycteropus afer*, means 'African digger-foot'. The bushmen believe that aardvarks have supernatural powers because they are literally 'in touch' with the underworld.

This elusive nocturnal animal probably only became known in the English-speaking world because it is so close to the start of the dictionary. It very nearly didn't make it. *Aardvark*, the fourth noun listed in the 1928 *Oxford English Dictionary*, owes its inclusion to the editor James Murray, who overrode his assistant's opinion that the word was 'too technical'.

'To aardvark' is US college slang for sexual intercourse (i.e. rootling around in dark places with a long thin part of the body).

Albatross
Flying non-stop for a decade

There are twenty species of albatross from the gull-sized Sooty to the vast Wandering albatross (*Diomedes exulans*, or 'albatross in exile'), with its record 11-foot wingspan. They fly further and for longer than any other family of birds. Satellite tracking reveals that some albatrosses fly around the entire planet in less than two months and can soar for six days without flapping their wings. Rather than soaring high up in the thermals like birds of prey, they keep close to the surface of the sea, using the lift generated by wind from waves. The most energetic part of any albatross flight is take-off: it is the only time the bird needs to flap its wings vigorously.

As soon as a young Wandering albatross gets airborne it won't land again until it is ready to breed, which can be ten years later. They feed on fish, squid and krill, either diving into the sea or picking it off the surface, and sleep on the wing, with each half of the brain taking it in turns to turn off.

> *Everybody commended them and ate heartily of them tho' there was fresh pork upon the table.*
>
> **JOSEPH BANKS**
> on board the
> Endeavour (1769)

Albatrosses belong to the order *Procellariiformes*, originally *Tubinares*, which means 'tube-nosed'. These tubes run the length of their large, hooked beaks and lead to very well-developed scent organs, allowing them to detect their food and nesting sites from many miles away. In some species the tubes have a dual function, allowing them to breathe from one part, while sneezing excess sea salt from another.

Young albatrosses spend several years watching their elders to learn the elaborate beak-clacking courtship dances. When they find a partner, they mate for life, developing a unique body language which they use to greet each other after long separations. They raise only one egg every two years, with the parents taking turns to sit on the nest or go off in search of food. An albatross will regularly fly 1,000 miles for a single mouthful for its chick. Solid food is regurgitated, but for longer journeys it can also be broken down into a concentrated protein-rich oil, kept in their stomachs. This can be used in place of water to quench their thirst, or regurgitated as a nutritious fish smoothie for the chick.

The albatross's most recognisable features are its huge wings. It costs very little muscle energy to keep them spread because of 'shoulder lock' – a special tendon formation that keeps them in place

Albatrosses can live for sixty years but breed so slowly that they are at risk of extinction within the next century. The main threat is long-line fishing. Over 100,000 die each year caught in the millions of baited hooks that are used to catch tuna.

Samuel Taylor Coleridge's poem 'The Rime of the Ancient Mariner' (1798) practically invented the myth that killing an albatross brought bad luck. In fact, British sailors regularly killed and ate them, making pipes from their bones and purses from their feet. A more widespread belief was that the albatross was the reincarnated spirit of a drowned sailor. Some Scottish fishermen still don't like using Swan Vesta matches because the bird on the box looks like an albatross.

When Portuguese explorers first saw them they called them *alcatraz*, their name for any large seabird. The word originally came from the Arabic *al-gattās*, the leather bucket on a waterwheel which resembled a pelican's bill. So, in Portuguese, the Birdman of Alcatraz literally means the 'Birdman of the Large Seabird'.

Anglerfish
Worse things happen at sea

Surely a life doesn't get any bleaker than that of the deep-sea anglerfish? Two miles down in the endless darkness, a gloomy motionless lump of brittle bone, atrophied muscle and paper-thin black skin with only luminous bacteria for company. A life spent doing nothing except waiting, often for months at a time, turning your light on and off in the hope that it will attract some other creature out of the inky gloom long enough for them to stray too close to your cavernous mouth . . .

The name 'anglerfish' is used for about 300 species — including sea toads, frog-fish, batfish and monkfish — which attract their prey with a long, flexible appendage like a fishing rod, typically growing out of the middle of their heads. At the end of it, in place of a dangling maggot, there is the *esca* (Latin for food), which can be wiggled to mimic live bait. In the deep-sea anglers, the esca lights up, thanks to a chemical

The male Photo-corynus spiniceps is the smallest known vertebrate, a quarter of an inch long, about half a million times smaller than the female.

process controlled by the bacteria that live on it. In return for light, the anglerfish supplies them with food. Different anglerfish have differently shaped escas. It was once thought this was to attract different prey, but it's now believed that they all have a similar diet. Perhaps having a big, bendy, glowing rod sticking out of your head is a form of sexual display.

The deep-sea anglers are some of the most ugly and outlandish creatures on the planet. They have an elastic stomach that can swallow prey twice as large as themselves (it even has a light-proof lining in case they swallow luminous fish). To prevent their prey escaping they have backwards-facing teeth in their mouths and another set of teeth in their throats. The female Illuminated netdevil (*Linophryne arborifer*) looks like a fluorescent root vegetable, with a black bulbous body and two shimmering lures streaming off like psychedelic foliage. Her Latin name means 'tree-shaped toad that fishes with a net.' The Hairy seadevil's (*Caulophryne polynema*) huge spiny fins have a decayed look, its body is covered in unpleasant pale hairs and its lure looks like a frayed stick of liquorice. It has one of the most sensitive lateral lines of any fish – the tiniest movement triggers the opening and closing of its jaws. Elsman's whipnose (*Gigantactis elsmani*) swims along upside down, trailing its lure along the seabed. The Wolftrap seadevil (*Lasiognathus saccostoma*, or 'hairy-jawed sack-mouth') has a lure with three shining hooks on the end that it casts forwards like a fly-fisherman. Prince Axel's wonderfish (*Thaumatichthys axeli*) has its lures hanging down from the roof of its mouth like a pair of fluorescent tonsils.

The male deep-sea anglerfish is much smaller than the female and doesn't have a lure. He's interested in mating, not fishing. He uses his giant eyes to look for a suitable female, and his enormous nostrils to sniff out her pheromones. Having found her, he latches on to her with his teeth and then starts to disappear. Scales, bones, blood vessels all merge into those of the female. After a few weeks all that's left of the male are the testes hanging off the female's side, supplying her with sperm. Females have been found with eight testes attached to their sides.

In some species, if the male fails to find a female, then he will eventually turn into one himself and grow massively in size. As the anglerfish themselves are wont to remark: there's only one thing worse than being an anglerfish and that's being a *male* anglerfish.

LOVE IN THE DARK

'Have you got a light?'

'Have you got the balls?'

Ant
Chemical-dependent

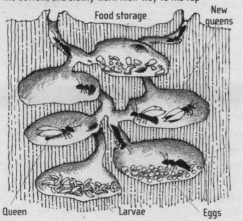

Ants boggle the mind. In the jungles where three-quarters of them live, they teem 800 to the square yard, 2.4 billion to the square mile and collectively weigh four times more than all the neighbouring mammals, birds, reptiles and amphibians put together. The 12,000 named ant species come in all shapes and sizes: a colony of the smallest could live happily inside the braincase of the largest. Like bees and termites, their success flows from their social organisation, but there is nothing remotely cuddly about ants: they are the stormtroopers of the insect world, their ruthlessly efficient colonies operating like a single 'super-organism'.

Every process within an ant colony is regulated by chemicals. In some species, this can be refreshingly direct: the queen will climb to a high point when she is ready to mate, then stick her backside in the air and release a love-pheromone that inflames the ardour of all males in range. Ant species mate in a variety of different ways: in mid-air, on the ground or in a 'mating ball', where the queen is completely surrounded by a swarm of love-addled males.

As well as love charms, phero-mones also act as air-raid sirens.

EARTHSCRAPER

Some ants' nests can be over 10 feet deep, with each chamber devoted to a different function. Ants are born at the bottom, and slowly work their way to the top

Food storage

New queens

Queen   Larvae   Eggs

If the colony is threatened, many species emit a pheromone from a gland in their mouths. This causes some workers to grab the larvae and run underground while others prance around with their mandibles open, ready to bite and sting. Brunei ants even have guards that explode their own heads when threatened, leaving a sticky mess which slows down the intruders.

Inter-species warfare is common and ant raiders will take hostages back to their own colony, where they become slaves. Other species use this to their advantage: the queen of *Bothriomyrmex decapitans* allows herself to be dragged to the nest of rival species, where, like a mini-Trojan horse, she bites off the head of the host queen and begins laying her own eggs. Being ants, the host workers switch loyalty without batting an antenna.

> *Harvester ants eat more small seeds than all the mammals and birds put together. Like squirrels, they often forget where they've put their stashes, so are accidentally responsible for planting a third of all herbaceous growth.*

Some ants raise livestock. They collect the honeydew made by aphids and in return protect them from other predators. The ants 'milk' the honeydew by gently stroking the aphid's abdomen with their antennae. Meanwhile, more than 200 species of ant are arable farmers, farming fungi for food. They gather compost for it to grow on, fertilise it with their dung, prune it and even fumigate it with powerful bacteria to keep it parasite-free.

But for all their awe-inspiring industry and adaptive élan, ants don't get it all their own way. The South American bullet ant (*Paraponera clavata*) is one of several species that finds out too late that fungi can sometimes farm them. Spores from a *Cordyceps* fungus work their way inside the ant's body and release an 'override' pheromone which scrambles its orderly world. Confused and reeling, it finds itself climbing to the top of a tall plant stalk and clamping itself there with its jaws. Once in place, the fungus's fruiting body erupts as a spike from the insect's brain and sprinkles a dust of spores on the ant's unsuspecting sisters toiling below.

Armadillo
The best-endowed of all mammals

If the male Nine-banded armadillo (*Dasypus novemcinctus*) were human, its penis would be 4 feet long. When you're making love to something that resembles an upturned fishing dinghy, size matters.

Describing armadillos has always been a challenge: the Aztecs called them *azotochtli*, 'turtle rabbits'.

All twenty species live in the Americas. The smallest is the Pink Fairy armadillo (*Chlamyphorus truncatus*), which is no longer than a sausage and looks like a furry prawn. The Screaming Hairy (*Chaetophractus vellerosus*) armadillo squeals like a pig when disturbed, though this seldom happens: it spends seventeen hours a day asleep and often won't wake even if you pick it up or hit it with a broom.

> During the Great Depression in 1930s America, hungry people resorted to baking armadillos. They were nicknamed 'Hoover Hogs' as a dig at President Herbert Hoover.

The Giant armadillo (*Priodontes maximus*) weighs up to 135 lb (heavier than most Texan cheerleaders), sports lethal 9-inch claws and has the largest number of teeth of any mammal: a hundred tubular pegs that never stop growing. The Three-banded armadillo (*Tolypeutes tricinctus*) is the only one that can roll into a ball.

Nine-banded armadillos (despite the handicap of having wedding-tackle big enough to scratch their own chin with) are strong swimmers. They swam the Rio Grande in 1850 and spread to most of the southern United States where

'Something for the weekend, sir?'

there are now between thirty and fifty million of them.

They have two ways of getting across rivers. Their bony armour means they naturally sink, so they can just stroll along the bottom, holding their breath for up to six minutes. If they need a longer swim, they gulp down air and inflate their stomachs into life-jackets.

Males mark their territory with urine and their smell has been likened to that of an elderly blue cheese. To avoid giving birth in the winter, females can hang on to a fertilised egg for up to two years.

> The poet Dante Gabriel Rossetti kept a pair of armadillos as pets in his back garden in Chelsea. One of them burrowed its way into his neighbour's kitchen – its head appeared from under a hearthstone and convinced the cook that she had been visited by the Devil.

Other than humans and mice, Nine-banded armadillos are the only animals seriously afflicted by leprosy: most armadillos in Louisiana are lepers.

In next-door Texas, armadillos are one of two state mammals – the other is the Texas longhorn. They've also been nicknamed the 'Texan speed bump'. Their singularly ineffective defence mechanism is to leap several feet in the air when startled: Texan highways are littered with them.

As a result, armadillos lead the world in research into the function of the mammalian penis. The members of dead armadillos are regularly harvested from road-kill – a job made easier by the fact that they are so gigantic.

Armadillos have been around for sixty million years: they are almost as old as the dinosaurs. In Bolivia and Peru, their shells are made into mandolins called *charangos* in imitation of Spanish guitars. They are then fitted with ten strings, generally tuned to A minor – a sad and noble key.

Badger
Woodland aristocrats

The parallels with the British upper classes are striking: badgers are stubborn creatures of habit; some of their setts, and the paths or 'runs' that lead to them, are centuries old, handed down from generation to generation like stately homes. The largest sett ever found was a veritable Blenheim Palace with more than 130 entrances, fifty rooms and half a mile of tunnels. Seventy tons of earth had been moved to make it. Most setts house a group of up to twenty adult badgers, known as a 'clan', and they will spend half their lives inside it, fast asleep.

Badgers are members of the Mustelid family, closely related to weasels and otters. 'Mustelid' comes from the Latin for weasel, *mustela*, itself from the word for, mouse, but badgers mostly feed on juicy earthworms, and very rarely need to drink as a result. If pushed, they will eat mice, as well as rats, toads, wasps, beetles, hedgehogs and even cereal crops.

Their stripe lets other species know that they are strong, fierce and ready to defend themselves. To communicate with their clan they produce a

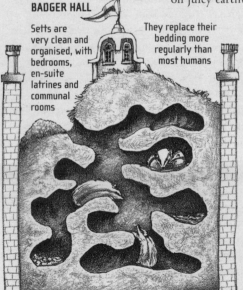

BADGER HALL

Setts are very clean and organised, with bedrooms, en-suite latrines and communal rooms

They replace their bedding more regularly than most humans

strong 'musk' from glands under their tails. This is used for marking territory and establishing family identity. Each badger has its own unique scent and a 'clan odour' made by the continual swapping of scent. Any adult that spends too long out of the sett risks rejection if his clan scent wears off. They have also evolved a vocabulary of sixteen different sounds, including churrs, growls, keckers, yelps and wails. Hearing the wail was once taken as an omen of impending death.

Badgers can mate at any time of year, and sex can last for up to ninety minutes. The sow will mate with several different boars, holding all the fertilised eggs until she gives birth to a multi-fathered litter in the early spring. Only 60 per cent of cubs will survive their first year of life. Most die by the time they are seven: 1 in 6 are killed on British roads each year.

Britain has the highest concentration of badgers of any country. Since 1985, the population has grown by 70 per cent to over 300,000, despite culling prompted by the belief that they spread tuberculosis to cattle. Paradoxically, culling badgers has the opposite effect. Since culling began in the 1970s, 59,000 badgers have been killed but more than 118,000 infected cattle have been slaughtered. This is because culling causes badger colonies to break up, forcing the infected survivors to move.

The European (or Eurasian) badger (*Meles meles*) spread into Europe from China two million years ago. They are still common there today. The hair for shaving-brushes originates on the backs of Chinese badgers, who are culled as an agricultural pest. Despite the myth, they are not shorn like sheep.

The origin of the word 'badger' is uncertain, but the best guess is the French *bêcher*, meaning 'to dig'. The French call them *blaireau*, a word they also use for 'shaving-brush' and 'tourist' (because of the well-worn tourist 'badger runs').

> Victorian gentlemen used the badger's penis bones as tie-pins.

Badger meat was once eaten in both Ireland and Britain. Their hind legs were cured as 'badger hams' and tasted like well-hung mutton.

Bat
Numerous, loud, well-groomed

There are a lot of bats. They account for a fifth of all mammal species and are more widely distributed, and come in a wider range of shapes and sizes, than any other mammalian order except the rodents.

Their success isn't hard to understand. They are the only mammal so far to sprout wings and fly, opening up a whole new world of habitats and food sources. Their order name *Chiroptera* means 'hand wing', and their wings remain recognisable as hands, with a thumb and four fingers. If ours grew to match them, our fingers would be almost 7 feet long and thinner than knitting needles.

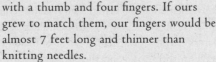

Tendons and muscles are arranged to enable bats to hang upside-down when roosting

The 900 species of bat are split into two families: the micros and the megas. The megas are the tropical fruit bats; the much more numerous micros are the echolocators. An average microbat emits 400,000 calls an evening. These 'chirps' have been measured at 110 decibels: louder than the average rock band, but at a frequency too high for us to hear. Bats prevent damage to their own ears by closing them with every wing stroke. They also use the energy from the stroke to force the air through their larynx, so flaps, chirps and ear muffling are perfectly coordinated.

Each chirp of sound can tell the bat the location, size, direction and even the

The bat spends no energy in hanging because their body weight automatically locks their clawed toes shut – even dead bats remain hanging

hardness of an object. It is accurate enough to detect a single thread of spider silk 3 feet away. Once locked on to prey the ultrasound speeds up into attack mode.

The largest-ever gatherings of mammals are the fifty-million-strong roosts of the Mexican free-tailed bat (*Tadarida brasiliensis mexicana*) whose 'evening;' evacuation has to start in the mid-afternoon to allow them all time to exit.

Inside the 'nursing' roosts, there are more than 1,500 babies per square foot, yet the mother bats use sound and smell to feed only their own offspring. The females 'conceive' while hibernating, warming up in their sleep as the wandering males caress them. The sperm stays alive inside the female until they wake in the spring and the eggs are finally fertilized

Bats groom themselves for an hour a day, rubbing their wings with oil from glands on their faces, to keep them moist and supple. They can live for thirty years.

Vampire bats (*Desmodus rotundus*) feed mainly on cattle, horses, tapirs and turkeys. If they do dine on humans, they usually go for the big toe, not the neck, but can only manage two table-

spoons at one sitting. They are the only mammals to live exclusively on blood. It is a relatively low-energy food, so if a vampire fails to score over two consecutive nights it will die. To offset this, they have developed a sophisticated system in which adult females feed one another. They even remember who has helped them and make sure they get repaid first. A blood-thinning drug developed from vampire bat saliva, called *draculin*, is used to treat heart attack and stroke victims.

Bat guano is valuable as fertiliser and is a source of saltpetre used to make gunpowder. It is also nutritious: a quarter-pound of it contains more protein and minerals than a Big Mac.

Bear
Sleep, eat, sleep, sleep, eat

Male and female bears are known as *boars* and *sows*, despite being about as closely related to pigs as koalas are to bears, or pandas to cats. The bear family's closest relatives are actually dogs, but one thing they do share with pigs is an omnivorous diet – most are as happy snacking on plants and fruit as they are gnawing on the leg of an elk. They can be fussy, too. Only a really hungry brown bear (*Ursus arctos*) eats a whole salmon. Most of the time it only goes for the high-nutrition bits: the brain, skin and eggs. And even the exclusively carnivorous polar bear (*Ursus maritimus*) has an odd liking for toothpaste. They have been known to raid Arctic tourist camps, knocking over tents and trampling equipment just to suck a tube of Colgate dry.

Bears spend much of their days eating, laying down fat reserves to get through the seven months they spend sleeping. Technically this isn't hibernation but 'torpor' because their body temperature, respiration and metabolic rate hardly alter. During this whole time they don't eat, drink, urinate or defecate but recycle their urea into protein and plug their anuses with a mixture of faeces, hair and bedding material called a 'tappet'. Female bears even give birth in their sleep: the cubs are tiny and premature and weigh a tenth of those of similar-sized mammals. As a result bear's milk is much richer than that of other carnivores and the cubs grow quickly. Newborn brown bears hum loudly while nursing, to help stimulate their mother's milk production. Each cub in a litter is quite likely to have a different father. Unsurprisingly, female bears have little or no post-coital contact with their partners.

Bears can sleep for as long as a month in the same position if not disturbed. All other mammals, including humans, suffer from osteoporosis (a thinning and weakening of bone) if they maintain non-weight-bearing positions for a long time, but bears recycle calcium into their bones and wake up just as strong as when they nodded off.

If someone offers you a slice of polar bear's liver, don't be tempted. A pound contains enough vitamin A to kill you. A smaller dose will merely lead to headaches, blurred vision, loss of hair, drowsiness, diarrhoea and enlargement of the spleen and liver.

The government of Yukon, as part of its official advice on what to do when you meet a bear, says that it 'can be dangerous to crowd a bear's personal space' – a statement which has about it the ring of truth. Brown bears can be black and black bears can be brown. Unfortunately, it's important to know the difference: if confronted by a brown bear, you should play dead. If you do that to a carrion-loving black bear (*Ursus americanus*), it will start to eat you. Not that you are in any serious danger. In the US, you are twenty-five times more likely to be killed by a snake, 180 times more likely to die from a bee-sting and 90,000 times more likely to be shot, stabbed or beaten to death by a fellow human, than to die at the paws of a bear.

FRUIT AND NUT CASE

Despite being the top carnivore across much of the US, black bears are 90% vegetarian

Beaver
Engineer, submariner, pharmacist

Beavers have a greater impact on their surroundings than any creature other than humans. They build instinctively: put a young beaver in a cage and even without trees or running water, it still mimes the process of building a dam. They can chop down a tree with a 6-inch diameter in less than an hour. Some scientists now think the disappearance of the Pennine forests and the creation of the Fens were due to the beavers that lived in Britain until the early thirteenth century (the town of Beverly in Yorkshire is named after them).

Beavers are rodents, like large squirrels. There are only two species: the Eurasian (*Castor fiber*) and the North American (*Castor canadensis*). Although similar in size and appearance the two have been separated for 24,000 years, so can no longer interbreed. They are larger than you might think. A fully grown beaver is the size of an eight-year-old human. The Giant beaver (*Castor ohioensis*), which became extinct 10,000 years ago, was the size of Mike Tyson.

Beavers can stay submerged for up to fifteen minutes. They have webbed hind feet, a flat tail to steer, transparent eyelids that work as goggles, fur-lined waterproof lips and closable ear and nostril openings to enable them to gnaw under water. The beaver's four incisors are bright orange. The enamel contains iron, for extra strength, and they never stop growing.

> Canada is built on dead beavers.
> MARGARET ATWOOD

Despite their 'busy' reputation, beavers can be rather lazy. During winter the average beaver only leaves its lodge once every two weeks. In spring and autumn the beaver's tail doubles in size. Beavers store their energy in their tails, so the tail shrinks as the fat is used up throughout winter.

In 1760, the College of Physicians and Faculty of Divinity in Paris classified the beaver as a fish because of its scaly tail. This meant that French settlers in North America could officially eat beaver during Lent and on other fast days. Beaver tail is supposed to taste like roast beef.

Beavers were once seen as walking medicine cabinets. The secretion of two glands near their bladder was known as *castoreum* and, from the ancient Greeks onwards, it was used as a fail-safe remedy for headaches, fevers, epilepsy and as a purgative. The Sami, in Lapland, mixed it with snuff. It is now only used in perfume. Shalimar by Guerlain and Magie Noire by Lancôme both contain synthetic beaver juice.

Beaver lips squeeze shut behind the front teeth to waterproof the submerged animal

The inner layer (dentine) wears out faster than the front enamel, creating a self-sharpening chisel effect that helps beavers speedily saw through wood

Unfortunately, the high value of castoreum and the fact that it sounds like 'castrate' seemed to encouraged belief in the myth, propagated by Aesop and Pliny the Elder among others, that a hunted beaver gnaws off its own testicles to escape.

It doesn't, but beavers were hunted nonetheless: in seventeenth-century Canada their pelts became a currency called a 'made-beaver' or 'M-B'. A gun was worth 132 M-Bs. At the same time in Britain, 'beaver' came to mean 'hat'. In 1628 Charles I declared 'nothing but beaver stuff or beaver wool shall be used in the making of hats'. Beaver hats weren't furry: their hair was ground, squeezed and heated to make water-resistant felt.

Canadian trappers tamed and taught beavers to catch fish for them

Bee
Do I know you?

The most sophisticated form of communication other than human language is the work not of an ape but an insect. Honeybees can tell one another the quality, distance and precise location of a food source by a complex sequence of movements and vibrations called the 'waggle dance'. And, unlike most of the dolphin or primate 'languages', we can actually understand what the bees are saying to each other (each waggle, for example, represents about 150 feet from the hive). The discovery of this in 1945 was enough to earn Karl von Frisch the only Nobel Prize ever awarded for the study of animal behaviour.

More recent research has filled out the picture. Bees have a sense of time; being able to see in the ultraviolet range makes them more attracted to some flower colours and textures than others; they can learn by experience. They can even recognise human faces. Given that many humans struggle with this once they've turned forty, it seems utterly remarkable in creatures whose brain is the size of a pinhead. Yet bees who are rewarded with nectar when shown some photos of faces, and not when shown others, quickly learn to tell the difference. Not that we should read too much into this. Bees don't 'think' in a meaningful way. There's no small talk; they only ever communicate on two subjects: food and where they should set up the next hive. The 'faces' in the experiment were clearly functioning as rather odd-looking flowers, not as people they wanted to get to know socially. Equally, a single bee, however smart, is severely limited in its appeal as a pet, when separated from its hive.

It's not hard to see why bees were sacred to the Greeks, Egyptians and Babylonians. Not only is the hive the epitome of a well-ordered society, it is also full of drama. A new queen, as soon as she's murdered all her sisters, takes her 'nuptial flight', in which she mates in mid-air with up to fifteen drones. All the drones die (their penises explode with an audible pop, leaving the end inside her as a rather ineffective plug) and the queen returns with enough sperm on board to stock the entire colony on her own. A queen can lay up to 1,500 eggs each day during her three-year lifetime. She is constantly fed and groomed by attendant worker bees. Very occasionally the chemical balance wobbles and female workers start to lay as well, but rebellions are put down ruthlessly and all the impostors' eggs are immediately eaten by fellow workers.

The species *Apis mellifera* also provides us with the only edible secretion, other than milk, that we can take from an animal without injury. Properly sealed and stored, honey is the one food that does not spoil. Archaeologists have tasted and found edible 3,000-year-old honey found in the tombs of Egyptian pharaohs. Honey is 'hygroscopic', meaning it can absorb and hold moisture so that any moulds and bacteria that touch it quickly lose their own moisture and die. But honey represents only a fiftieth of the true economic importance of bees. In the US alone, bees pollinate crops worth $19 billion each year. Without them there would be no agriculture: every third mouthful of food we owe to the bee.

AT THE COMBFACE

Queen lays egg in brood cell

Female workers feed developing larvae

Larvae are then sealed in brood cell when ready to pupate

Larvae turn into pupae in sealed cell

New worker hatches, ready to get to work

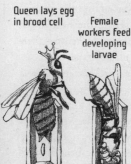

Beetle
The insect's insect

If diversity and adaptability are the measuring stick for success, then beetles are the most successful animals on the planet. There are 350,000 known species, with up to eight million more out there waiting for names: new species are being discovered at an average rate of one an hour. If you lined up all animal and plant species in a row, every fifth species would be a beetle. There are about 750,000,000,000,000,000 individual beetles going about their business right now.

Why are there so many? The simple answer seems to be flowering plants. Not much happened for beetles until the flowering plants began to diversify 120 million years ago. They were the beetles' food of choice and as they crept across the planet, adapting themselves to new environments, the beetles followed. In the process, they far outstripped even the plants; able to burrow, fly and swim, beetles became the universal animal. If something's edible, you can guarantee there will be a beetle out there to eat it. Ham, tobacco, ginger, bonemeal, paper, carpet, stuffed animals, strychnine, wood, all are grist to a particular beetle's mandibles. The 'short-circuit' beetle chews through lead sheathing on telegraph cables to get to the tasty fibre insulator around the copper wires. A specialist called *Zonocopris gibbicolis* feeds only on the droppings of large land snails, hitching a ride inside the shell.

Their mating strategies are just as varied. Flour beetles have even found a way of reproducing by proxy. When it's not

> Beetles are not aristocratic, vain esoterics, like butterflies and moths, or communists, like ants and bees. They're not filthy, opportunistic carpetbaggers like flies. They are professional, with a skill. There is nowhere that doesn't, sooner or later, call in a beetle to set up shop and get things done.   A. A. GILL

A BLISTER BEETLE HONEYTRAP

Larvae of the blister beetle form themselves into the shape of a female digger bee. Attracted by the pheromones, a male bee attempts to mate

Frustrated, the male bee flies off with larvae attached to chest hair

These larvae transfer to females when he finally gets lucky, and then on to the nest to feed on honey and young bees

chewing its way through the nation's stores of grains and cereals, you'll usually find *Tribolium castaneum* copulating. They are very promiscuous, even by insect standards. The male starts by using his spiny penis to sweep out a previous occupant's load, before unleashing his own. Unfortunately, his rival's sperm has a way of clinging to his tackle, so his next conquest stands a 1 in 8 chance of finding herself fertilised by a beetle she's never met.

We have much to learn from beetle. But far from being just a grotesques' gallery, they are a living laboratory, where almost every extreme has been tested, every obstacle overcome. The Bombardier beetles, who fire a boiling chemical spray out of their rears at 300 pulses per second, might help us to re-ignite jet engines that cut out during a flight. Tenebrinoid beetles from the rainless Namib desert, who can channel the morning dew into their mouths using the microscopic bumps and troughs on their backs, are being used to develop new fog harvesting technology; and the Jewel beetle (*Melanophila acuminate*) may hold the clue to early-warning system for forest fires. It has an infra-red sensor under one of its legs that can detect a fire over 50 miles away. Why? So that it can fly *towards* the blaze. It knows the smouldering tree trunks offer a rare predator-free opportunity to mate recklessly and lay its eggs.

Only a beetle . . .

Binturong
Smell my popcorn

High in the trees of southern Asia's tropical forests there lives the only Old World carnivore that uses its tail for climbing. Commonly called a bearcat, it is neither a bear nor a cat, but a member of the civet family. Civets are related to cats, but are also cousins to the mongoose and the hyena. The bearcat, or binturong (*Arctitis binturong*), gets its name from a Malaysian language that no longer exists and at first glance it's not hard to understand the confusion: it has the face and whiskers of a seal, the thick shaggy fur and flat feet of a bear, the tail of a monkey and the claws of a mongoose. And it's no tiny, scampering marmoset: it weighs 3 stones and is 6 feet long (imagine a golden retriever that can use its tail to climb trees). So, although binturongs spend almost all their life in the canopy, they tend to move around quite slowly, which sometimes leads people to mistake them for sloths.

The binturong tail is a 3-foot long, muscular fifth arm with a bare leathery patch at the end for gripping, just like a monkey's, although they evolved quite separately. Also, just like monkeys, they use their tail to pick and hold food as well as for hanging from branches. The tail is

DON'T TRY THIS IF YOU ARE A BEAR

Prehensile tail for balance

Rear ankles rotate so claws can grip trunk

Fleshy pads for traction

Five strong claws

powerful enough for them to walk down a tree trunk head first, or upside down along a branch to pick hard-to-reach fruit.

Binturongs live mostly on fruit and have a very sweet tooth; in captivity, they show a strong preference for ripe bananas and mangoes but have been known to wolf down marshmallows, muffins, apple pies and milkshakes. This tends to bring on a sugar high, leading to an hour of uncharacteristically manic leaping and running around before they collapse exhausted and sleep it off. Despite this, wild binturongs are genuine carnivores and will occasionally snaffle a bird or catch a fish (they are excellent swimmers).

> Several US colleges have sports teams called 'Bearcats' and refer to 'a mythical animal that combines the power and ferocity of a bear with the cunning and quickness of a cat'. They obviously haven't met the amiable binturong.

Like the other civets, the binturong marks its territory with a pungent oil. Civet oil was used for centuries as a valuable additive to perfume, collected from glands of civets and genets with a special spoon. The binturong has a large gland under its tail, and wipes it on branches, posts and other landmarks to leave a calling-card that lists precise details about sex, age and sexual status. Compared with some other civet species, the binturong's scent smells pleasantly of buttered popcorn. It's left by both males and females, although the female binturong wears the trousers: she is much bigger and – although it isn't quite in the hyena league – has a large penis-like clitoris. Both sexes have been hunted for their oil, and the male's penis bone is a valuable ingredient in traditional Chinese medicine, promoting virility and the conception of male children.

Unlikely as it sounds, the other reason binturongs are taken from the wild is that they make excellent pets; although presumably not indoor ones, because of their need to climb. They have become popular in the US, where a fertile adult can fetch up to $2,000. Apparently, they are easy to tame and the tail even acts as a built-in leash – they will grip your hand with it when you take them out for a waddle.

Bison
Seventy million killed in fifty years

The bison herds of North America's Great Plains formed the greatest mass of land animals in the history of the planet. They could stretch 50 miles long by 20 miles wide. By 1890, there were only 635 bison left.

The American bison (*Bison bison bison*) is commonly called the buffalo, although it is not related to true buffaloes. It migrated from Asia into America 400,000 years ago and is now the biggest North American mammal: adult males weigh a ton, are 10 feet long, and stand 6 feet tall at the humped shoulder.

Bison are the most efficient machines yet developed for eating grass. Their teeth are wide, to maximise the volume of each bite; and long, to stop them wearing out quickly. Forty per cent of their body weight is digestive tract: their fourth stomach chamber holds 600 pints but a mouthful of grass takes up to ninety hours to digest. Bison chew the cud like cows, but extract a third more nutrients.

Since the end of the last ice age, the bison's only predators have been bears, wolves and humans. Many archaeologists now believe that it was hunting by early humans that made them form large herds.

The size of the herds means an amorous male has to stand out. Successful males have evolved bigger heads and more powerful front legs and shoulders, covered in darker woolly hair. Rutting males run full-tilt at one another and clash heads: the sound carries for three-quarters of a mile.

> In medieval bestiaries, the European bison was known as the 'bonnacon' or 'vilde kow', which defended itself by spraying a jet of excrement over a distance of 80 yards.

BOOM!

Without bison urine there would have been no prairie: it transformed the fertility of the soil. The more bison, the more grass, the more bison. The fragrant bison grass, used to flavour vodka, thrives on bison urine.

It was the railroad that started the slaughter. The workmen who built railways across the USA in the mid-nineteenth century needed meat for food. At the same time, the British army decided 'buffalo' leather made the best boots. Hunters were offered $2 a hide (called 'robes') or 25 cents for a tongue. A full-time bison-hunter like Wyatt Earp or 'Buffalo Bill' Cody could kill a hundred in an hour. Shooting bison for fun from moving trains became a popular pastime.

It was all over by 1890. Only 1 in 5 of the slaughtered bison were put to commercial use, the rest rotted on the ground. The total contribution of the fifty-year 'buffalo trade' to the US economy was $20 million, a paltry 28 cents per animal.

Specicide led to genocide. The indigenous tribes relied on bison for every aspect of their livelihood. The US government encouraged the systematic extermination of the herd as the simplest way of ethnically cleansing the valuable prairie lands.

Today, the North American herd has recovered to 350,000. Most are photographed by tourists or farmed for food. With a third more protein and 90 per cent less fat, bison meat is more nutritious than beef. Cattle and bison hybrids are also bred for eating: they are called 'cattalo' and 'beefalo'.

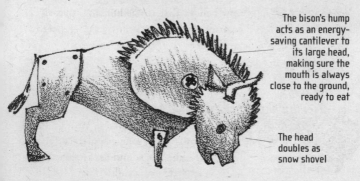

The bison's hump acts as an energy-saving cantilever to its large head, making sure the mouth is always close to the ground, ready to eat

The head doubles as snow shovel

Box Jellyfish
The stomach with twenty-four eyes

Despite appearing to be just a mouth surrounded by tentacles, box jellyfish or *cubozoans* (literally 'cubed animals') have eyes with lenses, corneas and retinas very similar to our own. Odder still, despite having all this sophisticated equipment, their eyes are permanently out of focus.

This is because a box jelly doesn't have a brain, just a ring of nerves around its mouth. Without central processing power, the blurry vision tells it all it needs to know. How big? Can I eat it? Will it eat me?

The eyes are on four club-like stems on each side of the cube-shaped body. As well as two 'smart' eyes, these stems each have four light-sensitive pits. Again, this is linked to their lack of a brain, which could integrate sensory information. For box jellies, 'seeing' a predator and knowing whether it's day or night are separate tasks which require separate sense organs.

Their eyes differentiate them from the rest of the true jellyfish clan (the *scyphozoans*, from the Greek *skyphos,* cup) from which they split at a

STING CELL TECHNOLOGY

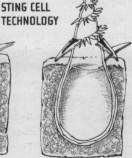

| Trapdoor opens when cell is bumped | Spring-loaded tubule of venom | Barbed harpoon shoots into prey at 45 feet per second |

very early stage, over 550 million years ago.

Box jellies go to bed at 3 p.m. and get up at dawn. Once darkness begins to fall they lie motionless on the ocean floor, apparently 'sleeping'.

Sight, however blurred, helps them in other ways. Unlike true jellyfish, which limply float waiting for food to swim towards them, box jellies can swim at speed (6 feet per second in some species) and steer around obstacles. This means they are able to 'hunt' prey. There is also evidence that they form mating pairs, with the male using his tentacles to impregnate the female, rather than just spraying eggs and sperm into the sea.

This also helps to explain their other major adaptation. Box jellies are fantastically venomous. One species, the sea wasp (*Chironex fleckeri*), is probably the most poisonous creature on earth. Its sting produces instant excruciating pain accompanied by an intense burning sensation. The venom attacks the nervous system, heart and skin, and death can occur within three minutes. Up to 10,000 people worldwide are stung each year, and there are regular fatalities.

Another species, *Carukia barnesi*, is almost as toxic. Virtually invisible in water, being transparent and no bigger than a peanut, it is completely covered in stinging cells. Those who survive its sting may suffer 'Irukandji syndrome', experiencing intense pain, nausea, vomiting, catastrophically high blood pressure and a feeling of impending doom. It is named after an Aboriginal tribe whose folklore tells of a terrible illness that struck people who went swimming in the sea. The venom causes a massive release of the fight-or-flight hormone noradrenalin, so victims often 'panic' to death.

Why are box jellyfish so toxic and how is this linked to sight? It's a question of scale. Because they can see, they tend to eat things larger than themselves. In order to minimise damage to their own rather delicate tentacles, they need to paralyse their prey immediately. They are only fatal to us because we are *so* large we blunder into them, exposing ourselves to far more of their sting cells than they usually need to kill their prey.

Butterfly
Souped-up moth

Butterflies and moths are the most numerous insect family after beetles, with 200,000 known species. Although butterflies are the more popular, carrying with them associations of sunshine and summer idleness, it's the moths who make up 80 per cent of the *Lepidoptera* ('scale-wings'). One of the reasons for this is temperature: butterflies are basically high-performance sex machines fuelled by flower nectar, Formula One cars to the moth's family saloon. If a butterfly's body temperature falls below 30 °C it can't fly and will either die or fall into a torpor. That's why northern countries like Britain are relatively poor in butterfly species – there are only fifty-nine natives and some of them, like the Red Admiral and the Painted Lady, migrate annually, all the way from the Mediterranean. In comparison, continental Europe has over 400 species of butterfly, and tropical Costa Rica (which is the size of Wales) has 560.

Moths are much hardier, and are usually nocturnal. Their bodies are designed to conserve heat rather than absorb it, so they tend to have fatter, fur-covered bodies and rest with their wings spread to the side, rather than folded together above their backs like butterflies. Another point of difference is the antennae: butterflies have a smooth antenna rod with knobs at the end; moths' are feathery. Again, this is partly to do with the day/night split. Moths are much less dependent on sight: they use their antennae as spatial orientation sensors, like our inner ears, to steady themselves as they fly and hover. Cut a moth's antennae off and it will immediately collide with walls and crash to the ground.

Sight is important to butterflies but not quite in the way we imagine. Despite their beautiful appearance, butterflies are extremely near-sighted and cannot judge distance. This is an evolutionary trade-off: their vision may not be sharp, but they can see almost the full 360 degrees, both vertically and horizontally, which is handy for evading predators. The bold wing patterns have more to do with scaring off hungry birds than attracting mates. What really gets a female butterfly going is the male's iridescent wing scales. These, arranged into the characteristic 'eye-spot' patterns, are ridged to reflect UV light – as he flutters his wings at close range he creates a UV strobe effect. Accompanied by heady gusts of pheromone, this literally mesmerises the female.

> Unlike most animals, none of the words for 'butterfly' in European languages resemble one another: it is schmetterling *in German;* papillon *in French;* mariposa *in Spanish;* farfalla *in Italian;* borboleta *in Portuguese* and vlinder *in Dutch.*

Moths, for obvious reasons, tend to rely more on smell and hearing: a moth can sniff a potential mate 7 miles way. Moths' ears are simple but effective; some species of tiger moth can even tune them to pick up the ultrasonic hunting call of bats and use their wing beats to create a jamming frequency. Both groups have scent scales, which release pheromones to attract females and help their own species recognise them. The Common blue butterfly smells strongly of chocolate; the Goat moth smells of goats.

SILKEN SECRET

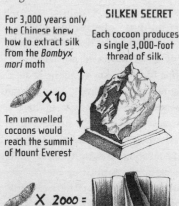

For 3,000 years only the Chinese knew how to extract silk from the *Bombyx mori* moth

Each cocoon produces a single 3,000-foot thread of silk.

X 10

Ten unravelled cocoons would reach the summit of Mount Everest

X 2000 =

A kimono uses 2,000 cocoons

Many species of moth feed on the tears of larger animals. Tears are a surprisingly nutritious broth of water, salt and protein – like our sweat, which butterflies like to lick. Some, like *Mabra elantophila*, are tiny and hardly trouble the elephants they steal from; others, like *Hemiceratoides hieroglyphica* from Madagascar, are large and sneaky: they have harpoon-shaped proboscises covered with hooks and barbs which they insert under a bird's eyelids as it sleeps.

Cane Toad
Alien invasion

On 18 August 1935, 102 cane toads arrived in Australia from Hawaii. The toads were released on to the sugar cane plantations of northern Queensland to control the ravages of the cane beetle.

Seventy years later, there are now a hundred million cane toads in Australia. They have spread into an area bigger than Britain, France and Spain put together and the front line of their territory expands at a rate of 35 miles per year.

Given the catastrophic decline of the world's amphibious species (see Frog), this may sound like good news. But cane toads aren't good news. They are a catastrophic example of what can happen when humans try to manipulate nature.

> Cane toads may yet prove useful: their tadpoles inhibit the growth of mosquito larvae and the venom contains serotonin, which can be used to treat heart disease, cancer, mental illness and allergies.

Bufo marinus is very poisonous. Swallowing them as eggs, tadpoles or adults leads to near instant heart failure for most animals. Australian museums display snakes that died so quickly the toad is still in their mouths. Native cats, or quolls, used to eating home-grown frogs, are threatened with extinction. Cane toads can even take out large crocodiles. Their venom is so strong that pet dogs become ill just by drinking water from bowls they have walked through.

In their home territories of Central and South America, cane toad populations are held in check by a combination of competition, disease and predators. In Australia there aren't any other toads, few predators and lots of new things to eat. It's virgin territory and they have risen to the challenge.

They produce four times as many eggs as native Australian frog species, and their tadpoles not only mature more rapidly,

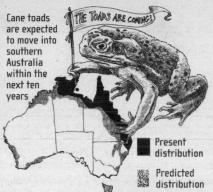

Cane toads are expected to move into southern Australia within the next ten years

THE TOADS ARE COMING!

■ Present distribution

▨ Predicted distribution

but – being poisonous – don't get eaten. Juveniles and adults will consume anything, from other frogs to unguarded bowls of dog food. The more they eat the bigger they get: some have been recorded at 6 lb – the size of a small dog.

Even more worryingly, their new home seems to be changing them. Their legs are now 25 per cent longer than they were in the 1930s and they can travel five times faster, waiting until the evening to use man-made roads and highways rather than scrabbling through the bush.

Action to control the spread of the toads is widespread, particularly along the border of Western Australia, where the invasion is expected in early 2008. Anti-toad measures once involved driving around so as to run them over in cars. Although cruel hands-on methods like 'cane toad golf' still have their advocates, the most effective control is through nocturnal 'toadbuster' squads which raid the waterholes where they gather. A good week's haul might top 40,000 toads. They are then either gassed or deep-frozen to death, and turned into liquid fertiliser called ToadJus.

A biological solution to the plague – genetically engineering a disease to render them sterile – is opposed by many environmental scientists, not least because it was that kind of thinking which caused the problem in the first place.

Despite its undeniable environmental impact, the cane toad has not yet caused any extinctions. Some birds and rodents have even learnt to flip them over and eat them by avoiding the poison glands. Many other species have grown to tolerate them, not least the sugar cane beetle, whose Australian population is, if anything, higher than it was in 1935.

Capercaillie
The fatuous grouse

Capercaillies, also spelt 'capercailzies', are huge woodgrouse as big as turkeys. The name is Gaelic for 'forest horse' – although there are no capercaillies (just as there are no snakes or moles) in Ireland. The Royal Society for the Protection of Birds gives the collective noun for capercaillies as a 'tok'. Interestingly, however, tok is not a word in Gaelic, Danish, Norwegian or Finnish – the local languages of some of the places where these birds are found nor, according to the *Oxford English Dictionary*, is it a word in English either. (Tok is, however, the spelling of 'talk' in pidgin English and a first name in Chinese. It's also a town in Alaska: pronounced toke, it means 'peaceful crossing' in Athabascan Indian. But we digress.)

The call of the male capercaillie imitates the sound of dripping water in early spring. It starts off with a similar *pelip-pelip* sound and then picks up speed with *plip-plip-plip-itit-t-t*, ending with *-klop!*, which sounds like a cork being pulled out of a bottle. The much smaller and less flamboyant females content themselves with a pheasant-like clucking noise. Male capercaillies perform a bizarre courtship ritual called a *lek* (from an Old Norse word meaning 'to dance') and they do this at so-called lekking sites. This involves strutting about with tails fanned out and wings held down, making an extraordinary series of noises including strangled gurgling, asthmatic wheezing and, of course, cork-popping. Some experts believe that there are also other sounds, below the range of human hearing, which carry for many miles, broadcasting the male's splendour to

> *Despite a valiant rearguard action by the RSPB, the capercaillie heads the list of British birds likely to go extinct by 2015. If it does, it will be the only British bird to have managed the feat twice.*

LEK LOUTS ON THE LASH

As well as all the gurgling, burping and cork-popping, lek fights between two males can be incredibly vicious, leading to severe injury and even death

The winner gets to mate with ALL the females; the frustrated loser withdraws and goes off to beat up other birds, cars or natural-history film crews

distant females. When the eager females arrive, crouching and making enticing begging noises, spectacular fights break out between the males, resulting in injury or even death. Those males whose grandiose exertions fail to find them a partner can become extremely frustrated and will perform their absurd antics to anything that moves, even cars.

Capercaillies became extinct in Britain around 1785, owing to over-hunting and forest clearances. In the 1830s, a few birds were imported from Sweden, and by 1960 there were 20,000 of them in Scotland. Today there are only about a thousand: the population has halved in the last five years and the bird is in danger of becoming extinct again. About a third of the deaths are due to the ponderous, low-flying creatures colliding with deer fences and a few of them, no doubt, from giving the come-on to moving hatchbacks.

The longest recorded lifespan of a capercaillie is 9.3 years. A 1992 study of deviant capercaillies in Finland found that about 1 per cent of males behaved abnormally due to testosterone levels up to five times higher than the average. This may be because capercaillies live almost exclusively on a diet of blueberries, a fruit that is supposed to increase the libido and cure erectile dysfunction in humans. Addled by blueberry-fuelled lust, Finnish capercaillies displayed to humans, attacked stuffed male capercaillies and copulated with stuffed females. In 1950, there were three times as many capercaillies in Finland as there are today. This may be because so many of them are stuffed for scientific purposes.

Cat
Cuddly killer

What is a cat? Every child knows. Yet cats, among the most familiar of animals, are ineffably mysterious. What are they for? What do they want? Cats spend 85 per cent of their day doing absolutely nothing. Eating, drinking, killing, crapping and mating take up just 4 per cent of their life. The other 10 per cent is used to get around. Otherwise they are asleep, or just sitting. They say cats were the last animals to be domesticated, by the ancient Egyptians around 3,500 years ago. But it is cats that have domesticated us, in their own time, for their own reasons.

Today, only a quarter of American cat 'owners' say they deliberately went out to acquire a cat; in 75 per cent of cases, it was the cat that acquired them. And studies have shown that many more people claim to own a cat than there are cats. When your cat disappears for a while it is not, in fact, off on a hunting expedition, it is next door but one having another free meal or asleep on the window-sill with one or another of its many doting 'owners'. Cats need to eat the equivalent of five mice a day. A cat given unlimited access to food will only eat a mouse-sized portion at a single meal. Is your cat eating five meals a day? Of course not: it's dining out elsewhere, later.

Most cats carry a parasite thought to have long-term, irreversible effects on the human brain. Toxoplasma gondii *may turn men into grumpy, badly dressed loners and women into promiscuous, fun-loving sex kittens. Half the British population are already infected . . .*

One of the big selling points of cats is that they are clean animals that carefully cover up their own faeces. Except they don't always – they only do it about half the time. They leave piles of the stuff all round the edges of their territory as a kind of malodorous 'Keep Out' sign. The polite word for this is 'scats'. Milk, cat food and central heating are all bad for cats. Milk gives them diarrhoea, cat food rots their gums and central heating causes them to moult all year round. Then they lick off and swallow their fur, which clogs up their digestive system.

There are about 75 million cats in the USA, which are responsible for the deaths of a billion birds and five billion rodents every year. Right up until the seventeenth century it amused people to stuff wicker effigies of the Pope with live cats and then burn the lot. This produced sound effects that pleased Puritans but not cats: they have exceptionally sensitive hearing and can even hear bats.

Research has proved what every cat owner knows: apart from human beings, cats have a wider range of personalities than any other creature on the planet. And yes, they are intelligent. Very. When they can be bothered. There are numerous well-documented stories of cats abandoned by their owners tracing them to locations hundreds of miles from home. Can cats map-read? Maybe. They can certainly tell the time, as recent experiments have shown. The ancient Egyptians worshipped cats as gods: killing a cat, whether deliberately or not, was a capital offence. When a cat died, its owner was expected to shave off his eyebrows. Whose idea was that? A cat's, of course. Cats don't have eyebrows.

ONE BLIND CAT

Cats can operate blindfold using only their whiskers

When a cat extends its claws, its paws double in size

Unlike dogs, they can move their digits independently and 'pre-form' their grip before they strike

'I told you we should have gone for the bell instead!'

Catfish
Swimming tongue

There are over 2,200 species of catfish and they are found on every continent except Antarctica. They live in the frozen rivers of Siberia and the steamy swamps of Borneo. Species have been found in the Himalayas and the Andes at altitudes of over 14,000 feet, while others bask in the warm coral reefs of the South Pacific. They range in size from some of the smallest known fishes to the largest. *Scoloplax dicra* is fully grown at half an inch while the European wels (*Silurus glanis*) grows to 16 feet and can weigh 650 lb.

Catfish account for about 8 per cent of all fish and are among the most remarkable creatures on earth. There is a talking catfish, a walking catfish, an electric catfish, an upside-down catfish and a catfish that looks like a banjo, but what really makes them stand out is their senses – the most finely tuned in nature. They have more taste buds than any other creature. Their entire bodies are covered with them. A 6-inch catfish may have over a quarter of a million taste buds, not just in its mouth and gills, but on its whiskers, fins, back, belly, sides and tail. The channel catfish has the best sense of taste of any vertebrate, able to detect less than a hundredth of a teaspoonful of a substance in an Olympic swimming pool full of water.

Catfish also have extraordinary senses of smell, touch and hearing. They can smell some compounds at a dilution of 1 part in 10 billion. They have no visible external ears, but because they are the same density as water, their whole body acts as a giant ear. In addition, ultra-low-frequency sound is picked

> Food historian and diplomat Alan Davidson once cancelled an official reception so he could travel north to taste and record a rare catch of the world's largest freshwater fish, the pa beuk or Giant Mekong catfish. He considered its flavour 'unmatched . . . comparable to veal'.

up by the lateral line, small pores along the fish's side containing tiny hair-like projections that are supersensitive to vibrations. These are used to find prey and avoid predators. The Chinese have exploited this talent for centuries, using catfish to warn of earthquakes: they are said to be able to detect them days in advance.

Catfish do not have scales – their smooth skin gives them a heightened sense of touch – and some also have excellent eyesight, especially the channel catfish (*Ictalurus punctatus*, Latin for 'spotted fish-cat') whose eyes are used for medical research into vision. Other parts are used to study herpes, their gonads are removed for research into reproduction and, if that were not enough, this unfortunate creature (variously known as the willow cat, forked-tail cat, spotted cat or lady cat) is also delicious. It ranks third after bass and crappie as the most popular fish to catch in Texas. As well as all the familiar senses, catfish – like sharks – have an extra one called electroreception that detects the electrical fields of worms and larvae buried in mud. Most catfish are harmless to humans (though some can give you a nasty jab with their toxic spines) but beware the *candiru*, a tiny catfish that lives in the Amazon. If you swim in its murky waters and urinate, the fish will find its way into your urethra. Once inside, it erects its spines, causing inflammation, haemorrhage and death.

THE MOUTHBROOD DIET

The male hardhead catfish hatches the fertilised eggs in his mouth

They take thirty days to hatch, and then use his mouth as a nursery for a further fortnight. Dad has to live on his fat reserves

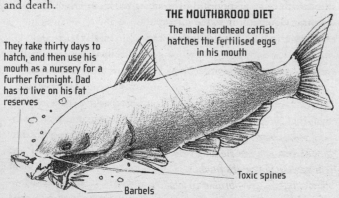

Toxic spines

Barbels

Cheetah

The savannah strangler

Cheetahs used to range across the whole of Africa and most of southern Asia. Over the past century, their population has shrunk dramatically as a result of hunting for fur and to protect livestock. Of the 12,000 surviving animals, only a hundred survive in Asia, in a tiny wildlife park in the Iranian mountains.

Cheetahs have almost disappeared before. The modern population can be traced back to a single African group of 500 animals that survived the last ice age. Genetically, this means all living cheetahs are as close as identical twins.

Cheetahs are fast because they have to be: unlike most big cats, they hunt during the day, climbing termite mounds to spot stray antelope or gazelle. The black 'tears' under their eyes are thought to cut down glare and they have a wide, super-sensitive stripe on their retinas that gives sharp focus across the entire width of their vision, allowing them to chase and turn with near perfect accuracy. Anything within a 2-mile radius is in trouble.

Only a handful of cars can reach 60 mph faster than a cheetah and none can do it on grass. But they have to be quick. Unless the antelope is caught within thirty seconds, the cheetah will overheat. They kill by strangulation. Their teeth aren't as long or as sharp as a lion's or a leopard's but their bite is more powerful, crushing the windpipe and blocking the airflow. If successful, it then has to bolt its food, leaving behind the skin, bones and intestines. An adult can take on board up to 30 lb of flesh in a sitting (equivalent to an adult human polishing off six legs of lamb) and survive on it for five days. Lions, vultures and hyenas steal half of all kills but cheetahs don't argue.

Ancient Egyptian tombs show paintings of the cheetah, which was revered as a god. Cheetah heads are even carved into Tutankhamun's funerary bed.

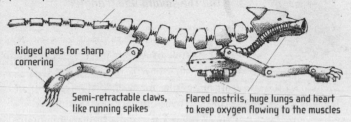

BUILT TO SPRINT

Long, heavy tail is used as a counterweight and the spine flexes to increase stride length (26 feet per stride, four strides a second)

Ridged pads for sharp cornering

Semi-retractable claws, like running spikes

Flared nostrils, huge lungs and heart to keep oxygen flowing to the muscles

They know a single injury to their 'fit-for-purpose' body will doom them to starvation.

A female cheetah will sometimes bring back a live antelope calf to train her offspring. Cubs start hunting at eighteen months and, untrained, will often chase after completely inappropriate prey like buffalo.

'Cheetah' is originally a Hindi word, *chita*, which comes from the Sanskrit, *chitraka*, meaning 'speckled'. There was confusion for a long time between cheetahs and leopards. When a medieval writer uses 'leopard' he usually means a cheetah. They were believed to be the illegitimate offspring of lions (which have manes)

> Cheetahs can purr, chirp and yelp, but they can't roar.

and 'pards' (which were spotted). Cheetah cubs do have manes (it helps camouflage them in grass). Their Latin name, *Acinonyx jubatus*, means 'fixed-claw with a mane'.

In ancient Egypt, India and Persia, cheetahs were trained to hunt by humans. Rewarded with butter and taught to recognise fifteen vocal commands, they were taken out on horseback, wearing hoods like falcons, and then set after antelope.

They are notoriously difficult to breed in captivity because the female needs to be chased by several males before she can ovulate. The sixteenth-century Mughal emperor, Akbar the Great, kept over a thousand cheetahs but managed only one litter. The next cheetah born in captivity wasn't until 1956.

Chimpanzee
The thinking man's ape

It is almost impossible to discuss the history of our nearest living animal relative without talking about ourselves. In 2002, a series of British TV adverts featuring chimpanzees dressed as a family of humans ended after forty-six years – the longest-running advertising campaign of all time. Their undeniable charm was based on a fallacy: that chimpanzees are like cheerful, uncoordinated human children. The irony is that the opposite is probably closer to the truth: that humans are chimps who didn't grow up. We got smart instead.

Adult chimps (*Pan troglodytes*) may not be much taller than a ten-year-old but they weigh twice as much and have five times the upper body strength of an adult human. Chimps can recognise themselves in a mirror, vocalise and use sophisticated gestures to communicate. Young chimps laugh when playful or being tickled. They appear to express emotions. They don't have the physiology for speech, but they can learn some human sign language – though without grammar or syntax. They can use a variety of tools – some 'fish' for termites with twigs; others crack nuts with rocks or sharpen spears with their teeth. They learn from one another. To this extent, different groups of chimps have their own 'cultures'.

'Chimpanzee' is from the Bantu kivili-chimpenze, meaning 'mockman'. It was first used by Europeans in 1738, although sixteenth-century Portuguese explorers called them 'pygmies'.

In particular, their sister species the bonobos (*Pan paniscus*), only identified in 1929, seem to approach the common problems of food distribution and reproduction from a much jauntier angle. Whereas chimp groups are run by a team of dominant males, bonobos are like a feminist hippy collective, with sexual contact – male-female, female-female, adult-child – used as the universal social solvent. Anything that arouses the interest of more than one bonobo results in sex. Unlike common chimps, bonobos often have sex face to face; like them, the males have huge testicles, because the females of both species are serially promiscuous. It's a sperm war: the more sex, the more partners, the better chance of raising your own offspring.

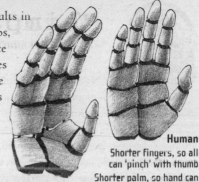

Human
Shorter fingers, so all can 'pinch' with thumb
Shorter palm, so hand can squeeze shut
Long powerful thumb

Chimp
Longer curved finger (branch gripping)
Strong knuckles (walking)
Short weak opposable thumb (limited tool use)

Here's a chimp power grip . . . look, no thumb!

All of this fascinates us, and why shouldn't it? Here are two species, closer to us than they are to the gorillas and with whom we share all but 1.5 per cent of our genetic material, whose behaviour is both like and completely unlike our own. But chimps and bonobos are no mere pit stops on the way to becoming human. Since our paths split from a common ancestor 5 million years ago, the genomes reveal that chimps have 'evolved' more than we have (meaning that more of their genes have changed as a result of selective pressure than ours). Also, they are much more genetically diverse than humans, suggesting that they were once common and we were rare. Whatever small genetic shifts allowed us to stand on our hind legs, freeing our hands to pinch and grip, and our brains to grow, it isn't a lack in the other species, just a difference. And, as Darwin once expressed it, a difference of degree, not of kind.

There are fewer than 200,000 chimps and bonobos left in the wild. The start of their decline predates human intervention, but we haven't helped: more are eaten as bushmeat each year than are kept in all the world's zoos. Imagine a world without chimpanzees. It's precisely because we can, and they can't, that we should save them.

Cicada
An insect that counts

Nobody really understands how they do it, but some species of cicada match their yearly life-cycles to large prime numbers, that is, numbers that can only be divided by themselves and one: 2, 3, 5, 7, 11, 13, 17, etc.

'Prime-number cicadas', or *magicicadas*, from the Greek *magos* meaning 'magician', are only found in the eastern United States and their nymphs spend years below ground feeding on tree roots. They only reappear to mate every thirteen or seventeen years.

The reason for this mathematical precision is to avoid even-numbered (and therefore predictable) breeding cycles, which their predators could match. By ensuring that trillions hatch on a single evening, but at unpredictable times, they literally swamp their predators, who gorge themselves until they can't face any more, without damaging the cicada population. There are thirty different broods, each of which is timed to hatch at a different time. The thirteen- and seventeen-year cycles only coincide once every 221 years.

In their long underground imprisonment, the larvae use their droppings to create waterproof cells, to help protect them from flooding. Even so, an estimated 98 per cent perish before they feel the urge to hatch. Those that do survive slough off their

CICADA HI-FI

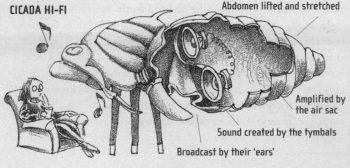

Abdomen lifted and stretched

Amplified by the air sac

Sound created by the tymbals

Broadcast by their 'ears'

childhood form and mate furiously. Most are dead within a fortnight, providing a huge nitrogen boost for the forest floor.

Cicadas are easily the loudest insects, but it is only the males who 'sing' and usually only on warm summer days. Some species hit 120 decibels, equivalent to standing in the front row of an AC/DC concert. They can be heard nearly a mile away. Cicadas don't rub their legs like grasshoppers, but make a series of clicks by buckling a pair of membranes, called tymbals, in their abdomens, in the same way we play a wobble board. Their bodies amplify the vibrations.

> Australian cicadas include the Green Grocer, the Floury Baker, the Double Drummer, the Cherry Nose and the Bladder.

They often sing in large groups, which makes it impossible for birds to locate individuals, but the main function of the song is to attract a mate (although some have a 'protest song' which they use if you prod them). Each species has its own distinctive set of calls, which the females' ears tune into.

The nineteenth-century French entomologist Jean-Henri Fabre tried to demonstrate that cicadas were deaf by firing a cannon towards a tree full of them. Their song didn't change, but not because they were deaf. The sound of the cannon was meaningless to them: you can't mate with heavy artillery.

Because of their apparent ability to be 'reborn from the ground' cicadas have come to represent resurrection and immortality in many cultures. In Taoism, they are symbols of *tsien*, the soul which leaves the body at death.

In ancient Greece, they were kept as pets. Plato tells a story of how they were once men whose devotion to music was so great that they wasted away, leaving only their music behind. Aristotle, on the other hand, was fond of eating them fried. Cicadas are still eaten across Asia and Africa and in Australia. Native Americans deep fry them and eat them like popcorn. They are surprisingly meaty and taste like asparagus.

Comb Jelly
Gooseberries with lovely eyelashes

Around 550 million years ago, animal life came in just four varieties: worms, sponges, jellyfish and comb jellies. The worms splintered into many different branches but the sponges and the jellies have changed little.

Early naturalists couldn't decide if they were animals or not, so Linnaeus compromised by grouping them together as *zoophytes* or 'animal plants'. Comb jellies are particularly plant-like to look at and their common names – sea gooseberry, sea walnut, melon jelly – have a distinct fruit & veg flavour. But they are unquestionably animals, and carnivores at that – gobbling up crustaceans, small fish and one another with what looks like single-minded dedication. Yet they have no brain – and no heart, eyes, ears, blood or bones, either. They are just a lot of mouth.

Most comb jellies are spherical or bell-shaped, ranging in size from no wider than a matchstick to longer than a man's arm. 95 per cent of a comb jelly is water; the rest is made of *mesoglea* ('middle glue'), a fibrous collagen gel that acts as muscle and skeleton rolled into one. To the casual observer, they look a lot like jellyfish: in fact the two are from completely different phyla and about as closely related to each other as human beings are to starfish.

The comb jelly phylum is called *Ctenophora* (pronounced 'teen-o-fora') from the Greek *ktenos*, comb, and *phora*, carry. Unlike jellyfish, which propel themselves by contracting their bodies, ctenophores move by rhythmically

> **Comb jellies are one of the ocean's most ethereal sights. The beating of the cilia diffracts the light, making the combs look like eight shimmering rainbows.**

beating their eight 'combs' – rows of many thousands of hair-like *cilia* (Greek for 'eyelashes'). Also unlike jellyfish, comb jellies don't sting. Instead, they have long, retractable tentacles covered in *colloblasts*, special cells that exude sticky mucus to trap their prey. They also have anal pores (real jellyfish use their mouths as bottoms) which nestle next to a gravity-sensing organ called a *statocyst* that tells them which way is up. While jellyfish can regenerate a missing tentacle, half a comb jelly regenerates into a whole animal. Comb jellies also have a simpler reproductive system. Most are hermaphrodites, capable of producing eggs and sperm at the same time (up from the gonads, out through the mouth) and – theoretically – of fertilising themselves. They generally just release thousands of eggs and sperm into the water. Their young can breed as soon as they hatch.

Comb jellies are thought to be more numerous than any other creature of their size or larger. They aren't great swimmers and are frequently swept into great, dramatic swarms, which pose a devastating threat to fishermen.

The collapse of commercial fishing in the Black Sea in the 1990s has been blamed on an American comb jelly, *Mnemiopsis leidyi*, that arrived as a stowaway in a US ship's ballast tank. Now known as 'the Monster', it can produce 8,000 offspring a day. The Black Sea population weighs over a billion tons, hoovering up all the plankton that once fed the local anchovies. 'The Monster' has also invaded the Caspian, threatening the caviar sturgeon. In 2001, a cannibalistic comb jelly, *Beroë ovata*, was introduced to hunt down and slaughter its beautiful but remorseless relative.

BEROE'S BLIND DATE

If the egg of a *Beroë ovata* is entered by more than one sperm, the nucleus takes its time to choose the sperm that fertilises it, sometimes going back to one it inspected hours earlier

'He loves me, He loves me not . . .'

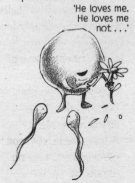

Coral
Sea skeleton

Corals share their closest family ties with jellyfish. It's hard to imagine two more different-looking animals, but they are both members of the *Cnidaria* phylum (from *knide*, Greek for 'stinging nettle'). Coral looks far more like a colourful, baroque relative of the seaweeds, but close examination reveals it as an animal, or rather a host of animals, as each frond is composed of thousands of tiny individual 'polyps', rather like miniature sea anemones (another relative). Each polyp has a fringe of stinging tentacles, a bottom-cum-mouth, and a stomach, just like their cousins. But they do something that the others don't: they build reefs, the rainforests of the ocean.

> Coral doesn't age as we do; most of its cells are the equivalent of stem cells in a developing human embryo, allowing even a small fragment to regenerate into a whole polyp. Some polyps may be over a century old.

By sucking in seawater, polyps extract the elements they need to lay down a solid base of calcium carbonate. This base is added to gradually, at about an inch a year, This provides a cup-like shelter for each polyp to hide in and keeps them moving upwards towards the light. Coral polyps 'grow' rock, in the same way humans grow bones. Eventually, as millennia pass, it becomes a reef, an intricate subterranean city where two-thirds of all the oceans' species live. If you gathered all the corals reefs in the world together they would cover an area twice the size of the UK.

Corals don't manage this all by themselves. They have evolved one of the most mutually beneficial partnerships on the planet, with tiny algae called *dinoflagellates* (Greek for 'whirling whips', which describes their method of propulsion), small enough to live, two million to the square inch, in their skin. The coral polyps catch microscopic organisms with their tentacles, and the waste products (mostly carbon dioxide) feed the on-board algae. In return, the algae give the polyps their striking colours, and produce most of their energy by photosynthesising sunlight. This is why you find most corals in shallow, clean, sunlit water. The algae even make a sunscreen that protects the polyps, allowing them to keep working all day. And it is hard work: reef-building corals use up proportionately two and a half times as much energy as a resting human.

Coral's relationship with algae is not without its tensions. If the algae can get food more easily elsewhere, as happens when the reef silts up or becomes too warm or polluted, they will leave, 'bleaching' the polyps white and condemning them to death. In the record-breaking heat of 1997 and 1998, a sixth of the world's coral reefs 'bleached'. It is now estimated that a tenth of all the world's reefs are dead, and if the carbon levels in the oceans continue to rise the rest will follow by 2030. Coral reefs are on the front line in the war against global warming.

Indirectly, coral helped Charles Darwin refine his ideas about evolution. Although he had no idea about the symbiotic relationship with algae, his first scientific book after returning from the voyage on the *Beagle*, published in 1842, was an account of the formation of coral reefs. He theorised (correctly) that atolls were formed by undersea volcanoes slowly sinking under the surface of the ocean, leaving the ring of coral still growing upwards towards the light. The long process of geological change implied by this con-firmed his hunch that constant change was at work all over the biological kingdom.

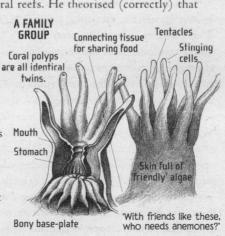

A FAMILY GROUP

Coral polyps are all identical twins.

Connecting tissue for sharing food

Tentacles

Stinging cells

Mouth

Stomach

Skin full of 'friendly' algae

Bony base-plate

'With friends like these, who needs anemones?'

Cow
Field factory

Watching cows placidly munching away in a field it's hard to imagine the fierce creature that so terrified Julius Caesar: 'Their strength and speed are extraordinary; they spare neither man nor wild beast which they have espied . . . not even when taken very young can they be rendered familiar to men and tamed.' He was wrong, as it turned out. Roman cows were the descendants of these same wild oxen, known as aurochs, which had originated in India and were first domesticated in Mesopotamia, 6,000 years earlier. Although sheep, goats and pigs were already being raised for meat, the domestication of oxen was a turning point: the moment farming became a business. Keeping cows was about more than feeding your immediate family. The word 'cattle' originally meant 'property' – cows were an indicator of wealth.

> Cows are fed magnets to cope with 'hardware disease', the damage caused by the bits of wire, staples and nails which they regularly swallow. The magnet sits in the first part of the stomach and lasts the cow's lifetime.

As a potential candidate for domestication, *Bos primigenius*, ticked all the boxes. It was large, ate grass and tasted delicious. You could say the same about bears, hippos and rhinos, but wild oxen herded together rather than ran away or attacked when threatened. And although bulls are fierce, the herd has such a strong hierarchy that most of the animals are used to being docile and obedient. Bears and hippos don't take orders. Nor do they produce gallons of milk, every day, without complaining. Cows quickly became our most reliable machines, converting rough grass into high-protein food and drink.

Cow farts are not destroying the world; unfortunately cow burps are. An average cow burps 600 pints of methane a day, and this is responsible for 4 per cent of worldwide greenhouse gas

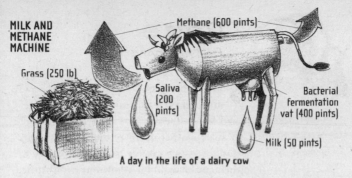

MILK AND METHANE MACHINE

Methane (600 pints)

Grass (250 lb)

Saliva (200 pints)

Bacterial fermentation vat (400 pints)

Milk (50 pints)

A day in the life of a dairy cow

emissions and a third of the UK's. Livestock farming in general creates 18 per cent of all man-made greenhouse gases – more than all the cars and other forms of transport on earth. Cows produce one pound of methane for every two pounds of meat they yield. Work is under way to produce a methane-reducing pill the size of a man's fist, called a bolus, which would dissolve inside the cow over several months. Even so, cattle farming is costly. To make one pound of beef requires 1,300 square feet of land, six times as much as to produce the equivalent weight in eggs and forty times what it takes to grow a pound of spuds.

On the other hand, cows have many uses beyond the obvious. As well as helping us tame disease through vaccination (*vacca* is Latin for cow), cows have put their whole bodies at our disposal. Pliny the Elder once recommended a concoction of warm bull's gall, leek juice and human breast milk as a cure for earache. Hippolyte Mege-Mouries used sliced cow's udders, beef fat, pig's gastric juices, milk and bicarbonate of soda in his original recipe for margarine. Cows' lungs are used to make anticoagulants, their placentas are an ingredient in many cosmetics and pharmaceuticals, and cow septum (the bit of cartilage which divides the nostrils) is made into a drug for arthritis. Their blood is made into glue, fertiliser and the foam in fire extinguishers. Brake fluid is made from their bones. Sweden even has a cow-powered train that runs on methane harvested from the stewed organs. One cow's worth will fuel a 2-mile journey, excellent news for the Swedish carbon hoofprint.

Crane

Oldest, tallest, loudest, highest

Cranes are record-breakers. The crowned cranes (*Balearica regulorum* and *pavonina*) are direct descendents of the earliest-known birds, whose fossils date back to the early Eocene, over fifty-five million years ago. The sandhill crane (*Grus canadensis*) holds the record for the longest surviving species of bird: a nine-million-year-old leg bone found in Nebraska is indistinguishable from that of a modern sandhill. The oldest recorded bird was a Siberian crane (*Grus leucogeranus*) called Wolf who died in 1988, aged eighty-three, in Wisconsin International Crane Centre. At six feet tall, the Sarus crane (*Grus antigone*) is the tallest flying bird and the Eurasian crane (*Grus grus*) flies higher than any other, reaching 32,000 feet. At that altitude, they are invisible from the ground, but are so loud they can still be heard.

There are fifteen species of crane and they are found everywhere except South America and Antarctica. Their beauty and elegance have enchanted human beings in every culture. They figure in prehistoric cave paintings, and Homer writes of their 'clangorous' sound in the *Iliad*. According to Roman fables, the god Hermes was inspired to invent writing by the letter shapes that flying cranes made in the sky.

Cranes seem almost human. They are sociable, mostly mono-gamous and spend years raising their

THE CRANE HORN

Sound travels over 3 miles

Cranes are one of the loudest of all birds and in most cultures they are named after their distinctive call

Windpipe (trachea) is very long and coils in their chest like a tuba

It is attached to the breast bone by a series of thin plates, like the bridge on a violin

Plates vibrate amplifying sound and allowing crane to control pitch

children. They have long memories and complex communication systems, using over ninety physical gestures and sounds.

They are also the avian world's best dancers, using elaborate choreography to develop social skills when young and for courtship when older. In a flock, once one crane starts dancing, all the others join in, bowing, leaping and running and even picking up small objects to toss into the air.

> *The demoiselle crane (Anthropoides virgo) is the smallest species, introduced to France from Russia in the eighteenth century. Their daintiness charmed Marie Antoinette and she named them 'demoiselle', meaning 'young lady'.*

There is evidence for imitative human crane dances from as early as 7,000 BC. In ancient China and Japan, among the Ainu of Hokkaido, the shamans of Siberia and the BaTwa pygmies of central Africa, the crane dance is a key ritual. Plutarch even records that Theseus celebrated his defeat of the Minotaur by dancing like a crane.

Cranes have also left their trace in language. Cranberries are named after them, from the similarity between the stamen of the plant and the bird's bill. The word 'geranium' is from *geranos*, Greek for crane: its seedpod resembles the bird's noble head. And 'pedigree' comes from the French phrase *pied de gru*, 'foot of a crane', as family trees look a little like birds' feet.

Eight of the fifteen crane species are endangered, two of them critically. In America in 1941, the number of Whooping cranes (*Grus americana*) dwindled to twenty but has since recovered to over 450. The breeding programme involves 'isolation rearing', where crane eggs are hatched and reared using hand puppets, humans in crane-costumes and taped calls.

Cranes were once widespread in Britain – almost every county has a Cranwell, Cranbourne, Cranley or a Cranford – but they are now Britain's rarest breeding bird. A tiny colony established itself in Norfolk in the 1980s, the first to do so in 350 years. Its precise location is a closely guarded secret.

Dog
Wolf with talent

The ancestors of dogs were the earliest known carnivores. Dogs evolved from wolves – grey wolves are their closest living relatives – and were first kept by humans between 12,000 and 14,000 years ago. It's not known whether it was a single event that spread, or if it occurred independently in different regions. While some think dogs invited themselves along by scavenging human rubbish dumps and becoming gradually less scared of humans, others think humans adopted wolf pups and that natural selection favoured those with milder temperaments. The famous breeding experiment by Russian scientist Dmitri Belyaev in the 1950s showed it took wild silver foxes only twenty years to transform into tame dogs (see under Fox).

> *The Fuegians . . . when pressed in winter by hunger, kill and devour their old women before they kill their dogs: a boy, being asked by Mr Low why they did this, answered, 'Doggies catch otters, old women no.'*
> **CHARLES DARWIN**

Today, there are nearly 400 breeds of domestic dog but all belong to the same species: *Canis familiaris*. In theory, a 2-pound Chihuahua only a couple of inches high can mate with a Great Dane more than 3 feet tall or a 150-pound St Bernard. The vast diversity of dogs is down to humans carefully selecting valuable inherited traits but often encouraging unusual ones such as dwarfism or lack of a tail that, in the wild, might prevent a dog surviving long enough to reproduce. Specialised hunting skills were especially sought after. Springer spaniels have the ability to 'spring', or startle, game. The dachshund's sausage-like body enables it to pursue badgers into their burrows ('badger' is *Dachs* in German). Labrador retrievers were bred to retrieve fishing nets in Newfoundland. There are Harehounds, Elkhounds and Coonhounds; Leopard Dogs, Kangaroo Dogs and Bear Dogs;

The now extinct turnspit dog or 'underdog' was a kind of terrier bred to work in the kitchen. It was long-bodied and short-legged, rather like a corgi with floppy ears. Turnspits worked in pairs, each doing alternate days

Pulley system attaches exercise wheel to rotating spit

Dog perpetually runs towards arnmatir hanging meat

there is even a Sheep Poodle. Poodles were originally used for duck hunting: the word comes from the German for 'to splash in water'. But dogs are bred for all sorts of reasons. Louis Dobermann, a German night watchman, produced his namesake for watchdog purposes in the late 1800s. Toy varieties, such as the Pekingese, were raised in ancient China as 'sleeve dogs' – kept inside the gowns of noblewomen to keep them warm.

There's no question about it: unlike cats, dogs are useful. A dog's nose has 220 million olfactory cells, humans a mere five million. A dog's sense of smell is not only hundreds of times better than a human's: it's four times better than the best man-made odour-detecting machines. Dogs can be trained to find almost anything by smell: explosives, drugs, smuggled animals, plants and food, landmines under the ground, drowned bodies under the surface of lakes. They can even smell cancer. Doctors in California have found that both Labradors and Portuguese water dogs can detect lung and breast cancer with greater accuracy than state-of-the-art screening equipment such as mammograms and CT scans. The dogs correctly identified 99 per cent of lung cancer sufferers and 88 per cent of breast cancer patients simply by smelling their breath. Dogs wag their tails when sad as well as when happy. Cheerful dogs wag their tails more to the right side of their rumps. Morose dogs wag to the left. Help them wag to the right: they deserve it.

Dolphin
Leave us alone

We haven't done dolphins any favours. The wilder shores of hippy speculation they have inspired – their brains are more complex than ours; their language is more sophisticated; they have a society dedicated to peace and free love; they are extraterrestrials with fins – reveal more about us than them. This is not to undermine their utter fabulousness, just to remind us that they are wild animals, with their own agendas and priorities. They can do things we can only dream of (and – just maybe – they feel the same about us).

Take echo-location, their system of marine navigation. Dribble a teaspoon of water into a pool and they will locate the sound with pinpoint accuracy. They can discriminate between objects made from wax, rubber or plastic. They can even tell the difference between identical-looking brass and copper

> *A dolphin's skin is shed and replaced every two hours to maximise streamlining.*

discs. Fish, not noted for their quietness (herrings fart non-stop), don't stand a chance.

Their 'language' skills are more difficult to assess. Dolphins are famously talkative – despite having no vocal chords. The clicks, whistles, groans, squeals and barks all come from sacs in their nasal passages – as many as 1,200 per second. Each dolphin has a unique 'signal whistle', an 'I'm Flipper' tag, which it repeats constantly. They also imitate other dolphins as a way of gaining their attention, rather in the same way as doing an exaggerated impression of a friend in a crowded bar means they are more likely to turn round. The whistle signals show that they communicate, but they are a long swim away from being a language.

Dolphin play is highly complex, and they learn fast. They have a striking ability to follow extraordinarily complicated human commands, and can recognise themselves in a mirror. They can even use tools: when hunting among sharp coral they attach bits of sponge to their snouts as safety masks. Legends of their helpfulness to gods and humans are threaded through Greek and Roman myth and contemporary accounts of dolphin 'rescues' are common. In small fishing communities, dolphins are known to herd shoals of fish into nets in return for a few thrown back and a friendly wave. It's hard not to love their big smiley faces.

But there is another side. For all the foreplay and nuzzling, females are frequently coerced into sex by groups of males. Schools of dolphins batter porpoises to death for no obvious reason, and occasionally practise infanticide. In a comprehensive study of wild dolphins that seek out human company, three-quarters showed aggression, which sometimes led to serious injury, and half indulged in 'mis-directed sexual behaviour' with buoys and boats as well as humans. Given that an average male bottlenose weighs 40 stone and has a foot-long, solid muscle penis that ends in a prehensile hook agile enough to catch an eel, you wouldn't want to give off the wrong signals.

This same report concluded that contact with us almost always means injury and suffering for the wild dolphin. It's worth bearing that in mind when considering the benefits of 'wildlife tourism' and 'dolphin therapy'. Of course, the idea of 'swimming with dolphins' is attractive and there is evidence that it does have therapeutic value. But we gain just as much (and maybe more) by standing on a boat watching them through binoculars, revelling in the fact that they are where they belong, doing what they do best.

NOSE SONAR

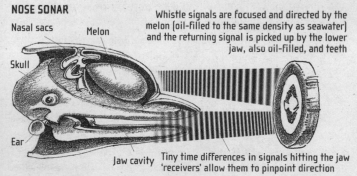

Whistle signals are focused and directed by the melon (oil-filled to the same density as seawater) and the returning signal is picked up by the lower jaw, also oil-filled, and teeth

Nasal sacs

Melon

Skull

Ear

Jaw cavity

Tiny time differences in signals hitting the jaw 'receivers' allow them to pinpoint direction

Donkey
A natural source of Viagra

Donkeys' milk is a wonder substance. Country people in India have always sworn by it as a baby food, but chemical analysis has recently revealed it is full of oligo-saccharides, carbohydrates with powerful immuno-stimulant properties. It has been tested in cases of AIDS and cancer, and some claim the milk has an effect similar to Viagra.

Donkeys were first domesticated in Ethiopia and Somalia about 6,000 years ago. The modern donkey is the same species as the African wild ass (*Equus asinus*). It is the only domesticated animal to have originated in Africa. They were used for transport long before horses, which were originally bred in Asia purely for their meat.

Ancient Egyptian tombs show that donkeys were the Porsches of the Nile delta: the more donkeys, the higher your status. Herds of a thousand or more were not uncommon. With donkeys came trade: their ability to carry 30 per cent of their body weight without complaint opened up the ancient world.

The word 'donkey' is surprisingly recent – it wasn't around when the King James Version of the Bible was written in 1611 – and probably originated in the late eighteenth century to avoid the growing confusion between 'ass' and 'arse'. According to the *Oxford English Dictionary*, 'donkey' was originally pronounced to rhyme with 'monkey' and is thought to come from 'dun', meaning brown or grey.

A male donkey is called a jack or jackass; a female donkey is called a jenny or donkeyess. The personality of a donkey is called their donkeyship.

Donkeys have sixty-two chromosomes (sixteen more than humans) and can be crossed with horses or zebras. The offspring of a male donkey and a female horse is called

The original desert truck

a mule. The male mule is called a john and a female mule a molly. The offspring of a male donkey and a female horse is called a hinny. Zebras crossed with donkeys are called zeebrasses and zonkeys. Only 1 in 10,000 of these hybrids are fertile.

Donkeys have a reputation for stubbornness; in fact, they are highly sensitive to danger and rather sensible. Unlike horses, which bolt when spooked, donkeys stand rooted to the spot, braying loudly, and are the only animals of their size that won't back down when confronted by a lion. In Africa, guard-donkeys are used to protect cattle. Dogs are instinctively scared of donkeys: they have a surprisingly accurate kick.

By 1939, there were only a hundred donkeys left in England. There are now about 10,000 – 800 are licensed to work on beaches and 75 per cent of them live in donkey sanctuaries.

Donkeys use their ears to communicate and cool down. They are much longer than a horse's (hence the phrase 'donkey's years' – a corrupted version of 'donkeys' ears')

Every donkey has a dark cross on its back that is supposed to date from Christ's entry into Jerusalem. Before it became associated with Christ, the donkey was identified with the Egyptian sun god Ra, and Dionysus, the Greek god of wine and theatre. Until the mid-nineteenth century, Santa Claus always rode a donkey.

Dead donkeys are lucky. You should jump over them three times. Or make a sandwich out of their hair to cure a cough. Or sprinkle their toenail clippings over your enemies. Or pop their heads in the oven: *cephaleonomancy* is divination using a roast donkey's head. In 1869 a donkey was served for dinner at high table in Sidney Sussex College, Cambridge. One of the dons remarked that it tasted 'rather like swan'.

Eagle
Omnipotent omnivore

Eagles belong to the family *Accipitridae*, from the Latin *accipiter*, a 'bird of prey'. In English, an accipiter is a 'nose-bandage' from its resemblance to the beak or claw of a hawk. Not everyone agrees what an eagle is; no one knows how eagle species are related to one another and the evolution of eagles is poorly understood. Eagles are defined by what they are not. According to one professional definition, an eagle is 'a large or very large diurnal raptor which is not a kite, vulture, hawk, buzzard or falcon'. In all eagle species, females are larger than males: the more aggressive the species, the larger the discrepancy.

An eagle's eye can be up to twenty times larger in proportion to its body than a human eye. They are so big in their sockets that there is little room for them to move: like owls, an eagle has to move its whole head to look round. Nonetheless, the visual acuity of an eagle is up to eight times better than a human's. An eagle can spot a

> Eagles lay clutches of two eggs, but the first chick to hatch usually kills its sibling, even when food is abundant. No one knows why.

rabbit from 2 miles away. As an eagle swoops down on its prey, the muscles in its eyes continually adjust the curvature of the lens to maintain sharp focus and accurate depth perception throughout the attack. Eagles of the soaring variety must wait until the air is warm enough to create thermals. The heavier the eagle, the later in the day it begins to hunt. Eagles, however, can hardly be described as heavy. A golden eagle (*Aquila chrysaetos*) is 7½ feet wide but weighs less than 9 pounds. A bald eagle's (*Haliaeetus leucocephalus*) feathers weigh more than twice as much as its bones. An eagle's dive reaches speeds of 200 mph, but only about one in four such attacks are successful.

Some eagles have given up on the exhausting business of

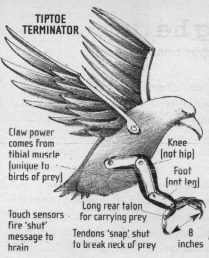

TIPTOE TERMINATOR

Claw power comes from tibial muscle (unique to birds of prey)

Knee (not hip)

Foot (not leg)

Long rear talon for carrying prey

Touch sensors fire 'shut' message to brain

Tendons 'snap' shut to break neck of prey

8 inches

roaming the azure yonder, falling like a stone and missing. They prefer to sit about biding their time. Many reptile-eating (and some fish-eating) eagles perch in trees in a lordly manner, waiting for their prey to scuttle by. They then drop straight onto them from a sitting position. The lesser-spotted eagle (*Aquila pomarina*) neither falls like a thunderbolt nor watches imperiously. It walks around looking for frogs to eat. Eagles will eat anything, dead or alive. Not just rodents, reptiles, birds and fish but ants, termites, dead elephants and whales, locusts, baby seals, crabs, snails, sloths, snakes and monkeys. Martial eagles (*Polemaetus bellicosus*) eat baboons. Golden eagles enjoy caribou calves. Steller's sea eagle (*Haliaeetus pelagicus*) is partial to seal pups. Crowned hawk eagles (*Stephanoaetus coronatus*) eat mandrill monkeys and can kill a bushbuck four times their own size. Both serpent eagles and snake eagles catch snakes. Serpent eagles fly off with the snake dangling from their legs, whereas snake eagles swallow them whole, head first. They then fly back to the nest, where the snake eaglet grasps the tail of the snake and hauls it out of its parent's mouth like a string of handkerchiefs. On a less grisly note (and despite its unnerving name), the favourite food of the Vulturine fish eagle (*Gypohierax angolensis*) is fruit from the oil-palm tree.

The two-headed eagle featured on many European flags was a symbol of the Byzantine empire: one head represented ancient Rome, the other, 'new Rome', or Constantinople.

Echidna
Spiny not-anteater

What has a bird-like beak, spines like a hedgehog, the eggs of a reptile, the pouch of a marsupial, the life span of an elephant and a penis like a four-staved club? Enter the echidna, Australia's almost-anteater. Like anteaters the echidna has a long sticky tongue, powerful front legs and a huge appetite for social insects. But there the similarities end. The echidnas aren't even marsupials, they're monotremes ('one-holed' creatures), so named because, like birds and reptiles, they have a single hole or cloaca for excretion and reproduction. Along with the platypus, the four species of echidnas are thought to be the only descendants of the southern mammals that split from their northern counterparts before the super-continent known as Pangaea began to break apart, 180 million years ago in the Jurassic. This makes them the oldest surviving mammal group.

The Short-beaked echidna (*Tachyglossus aculeatus* – 'thorny fast-tongue') is the most widely distributed mammal in Australia. They are shy, solitary creatures that live in large undefended territories (no one has observed an echidna fight). They have two predator-escape

> An echidna's neocortex, associated with reasoning and personality in humans, accounts for half the volume of its brain, compared to only a third in the 'higher' mammals. No one knows what echidnas use it for.

strategies: the spiky ball and the sinking ship (echidnas can dig straight down until only their spines are showing). They have the coldest blood temperature of any mammals, and can conserve energy by dropping their body temperature to 4° C and taking only one breath every three minutes. To warm up, they can lie flat like a spiny rug in the sunshine. To cool down, it is thought that their spines dissipate heat like an elephant's ears. They can live for fifty years.

Mating takes place in the winter when a group of males form a slow-moving 'love train' behind a pheromone-emitting female. This shuffling procession can last for more than a month. As soon as she's ready, the female clings to a tree trunk with her forelimbs while the males dig a 10-inch deep, doughnut-shaped trench around the tree.

THE EGG & POUCH TRICK

The female echidna sits on her rump, curls forward and pops her egg into her pouch from her bottom

They then compete for mating honours, gently pushing each other around with their heads. The winner lies on his side in the trench partly underneath the female and, unsheathing his curiously configured member, mates, pressing his belly against hers. A single grape-sized egg follows three weeks later, hatching a wriggling, bean-like 'puggle'. After eight weeks of rapid growth, the puggle is transferred to a burrow, just as the spines start to show.

As for the other species, there can be few animals more mysterious than the Long-beaked echidna (*Zaglossus bruijni* – 'de Bruijn's long-tongue') of New Guinea. Here's all we know: its body and nose are twice the size of its cousin's; it's furrier; it mainly eats earthworms speared with special spines on its tongue and then sucked up like spaghetti; it's nocturnal; it snuffles a lot. That's it: everything else is conjecture. We think there are three subspecies: one (rather sweetly named after Sir David Attenborough) is restricted to a single (dead) specimen, found in 1961. The other two are endearing, inquisitive creatures that look like four-legged kiwis and tame easily. This has made them easy to hunt, and since the arrival of Europeans, the taboo against killing a once sacred animal has disintegrated. Papuan tribesmen track them with dogs and serve them roasted as a delicacy. How many are left? We have no idea . . .

Eel
Freudian slippery

Nobody knows where the word eel comes from. Until the 1920s, nobody knew where eels themselves came from. Aristotle insisted they arose spontaneously from rotting seaweed. Pliny the Elder thought they rubbed against rocks and that the shreds of their skin came to life. Other imaginative suggestions included the dew of May mornings, the gills of fish, and horsehairs falling into the water. The astonishing life-cycle of the eel was first revealed to the world by the Danish oceanographer Johannes Schmidt (1877–1933) who, in 1905, was commissioned by his government to locate their spawning grounds. Given one small ship, he set off to trawl the oceans of the world. It took him sixteen years.

It seems all European and American freshwater eels (*Anguilla anguilla*) are born as saltwater fish in the Sargasso Sea, a strangely calm area of the North Atlantic around Bermuda, two million square miles in extent and clogged with Sargassum weed. This is kept afloat by berry-like bladders: hence the name from *sargaço*, an old Portuguese word for 'grape'. From here, the eel larvae are carried by the Gulf Stream 3,000 miles across the Atlantic to Europe, where, on entering the mouths of rivers, they miraculously transform into freshwater creatures. They don't aim at a particular river: they hit the coast in a broad band and swim up whichever one they encounter – so rivers with wide west-facing estuaries like the Severn get lots of them. They will go to any lengths to reach their goal, piling up their bodies by the tens of thousands to climb over obstacles. Once there, the eels live contentedly in

Eels are one of very few species of fish that can swim backwards. Their thick coating of mucus means they can also travel on land as well as in water. They make their way into fields and gardens to snack on young peas and beans.

rivers until they reach maturity. When this happens (between the ages of six and forty) they prepare to swim back to the Sargasso Sea again. They change dramatically. Backs turn darker; bellies turn silver. They toughen up, storing fat, which they'll need for the journey. Eyes enlarge, heads become pointed, nostrils dilate, the salt content in their bodies reduces and their sex organs swell. Their gas bladder also changes to allow them to withstand pressures of a ton per square inch.

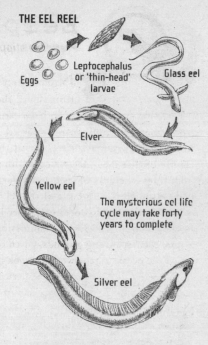

THE EEL REEL

Eggs

Leptocephalus or 'thin-head' larvae

Glass eel

Elver

Yellow eel

The mysterious eel life cycle may take forty years to complete

Silver eel

Once back in the Sargasso, the females spawn and the males fertilise the eggs, after which they all die of exhaustion. Or so it is believed. Nowadays, 'everybody knows' that eels are born in the Sargasso Sea but this has never been proved. No one has ever seen an eel spawn or seen one die there. Careful scientists prefer to call the Sargasso Sea the eel's 'presumed' breeding ground. Young eels have been found there, but neither live adults nor their eggs. Not one eel has ever been bred in captivity. When you catch an eel, its reproductive system shuts down completely, as if deliberately keeping the secret. Sigmund Freud was determined to find the answer. He worked in Trieste cutting up hundreds of eels to see how their sexual organs worked. When he had finished, he published a thesis in which he concluded that all of his research was a waste of time. He was no nearer to understanding eels than when he first started.

Elephant
A giant hamster on tiptoe

Elephants are the largest living land animals and size is both the secret of their success and the reason they look the way they do. Elephants grew big to compete with the waves of antelopes and other ruminants munching their way across the grassy plains. To eat the coarse, woody vegetation the ruminants couldn't manage required a big digestive tract and long legs. So they got bigger and by about two million years ago had spread all over the planet except Australasia and Antarctica.

Size brought its challenges. Overheating is a problem for large mammals: the elephant's ears evolved to stop it boiling to death. Unlike the thick skin that covers most of their bodies, the skin on their ears is paper-thin. Each ear is the size of a single-bed sheet and when it flaps, the airflow reduces blood temperature by up to 5° C. The skein of blood vessels acts like the grill in a car's radiator. The pattern they make is unique to each elephant and can be used to identify them, like human fingerprints.

Elephants' tusks are large canine teeth – chewing teeth are nestled deep inside

The other challenge is drinking, as kneeling down makes even a large animal vulnerable to attack. Elephants evolved the perfect solution, a 7-foot, 28-stone nose that contains a hundred times more muscles than we have in our entire bodies. Not only can a trunk suck up 8 pints of water, it also functions as an arm, hand, snorkel and weapon. It is powerful enough to kill a lion with a single blow, yet the finger-like lobes at the end can pick up a grain of rice.

Despite weighing over 3 tons, elephants still walk on tiptoe, like most mammals, but they are the only mammals with four forward-facing knees, needed to give them extra leverage when standing up. They can't run or jump (to 'run' all feet must be off the ground at once) but they can walk silently, reaching a top speed of 15 mph. They also use their feet to hear, picking up the very low frequency calls (inaudible to humans) of other elephants from as far away as 6 miles. Males and females can't understand each other's calls, and the female vocabulary is much larger.

The 'silent walk' is due to a layer of cartilage in their feet between the bone and the pad that acts as a shock absorber, with the outside of the pad hitting the ground before the centre. The sound produced when the pad hits the ground is trapped in the air pocket under the foot

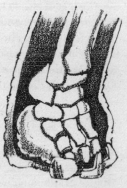

Elephants are large-brained and clever: along with dolphins and some primates, they are the only animals that can recognise themselves in a mirror. They spend twelve years as calves and their development involves a lot of learnt behaviour – a young elephant has to be shown how to use its trunk. They have elaborate mourning practices and often visit and fondle the bones and tusks of the dead. The oldest elephant ever recorded was eighty years old, but most live for about fifty years. With few predators (other than man), the default elephant death is starvation caused by their teeth wearing out.

The closest living relatives of the elephants are the sea cows, and then the hyraxes, furry creatures that look like large hamsters. The common ancestor of all three was a giant hyrax, Africa's primary herbivore until the ruminants arrived and set one branch of the family on the way to sprouting trunks.

An elephant's gait is a bit like Groucho Marx's: crouching slightly seems to help them to move their bodies more smoothly.

Ferret
Dancing Prozac

Ferrets are the only member of the weasel family to have been domesticated and their popularity as pets is on the increase. On the face of it, this is surprising. Their scientific name, *Mustela putorius furo*, translates as 'musk-bearing stinking, thief', although most of this infamy is inherited. Ferrets are tame European polecats (from *poule chat*, 'poultry cat'), a creature so despised by farmers and gamekeepers that it was hunted, trapped and gassed to near-extinction across most of Britain during the nineteenth century. Also known as the 'foulmart' or 'stinkmarten', the polecat was the scourge of hen-houses, but also helped keep the rabbit and mouse population in check. When they were originally domesticated, over 2,000 years ago, it was to exploit this natural aptitude.

> *Until the 1960s, ferrets were used to carry cable to inaccessible areas of Boeing aircraft as they were being built. They were replaced, as they often gave up and fell asleep halfway.*

Polecats and ferrets continue to hybridise easily, and, ironically, it is the wild 'polecat' streak that makes the ferret a wonderful pet. Unlike dull, grass-chewing, social rodents, like hamsters and guinea pigs, the domestic ferret has remained a solitary hunter, as pure a carnivore as the domestic cat. But ferrets have none of the aloofness of cats: they are as curious, bold and responsive as puppies. You can teach a ferret to come to its name or take it for walks on a lead. The inquisitive streak that makes it lethal in a rabbit burrow is hugely diverting when it's 'ferreting' around in the backyard. One particular manoeuvre, the 'war dance', involves the ferret leaping backwards and sideways, chirping with excitement. They are particularly valued as pets by single professionals, as they sleep for eighteen hours, make hardly any noise, but are always ready with a cheerful fuss when you do return home.

There are downsides. Despite keeping their quarters very clean, they do smell and even a well-looked-after ferret is probably a little too feral for indoors. Also, their natural high spirits mean they have little in the way of common sense. In a house they will disappear in holes in walls, behind doors, into cupboards, down the back of sofas and appliances like dishwashers, where they can get squashed. Nor do they have a homing instinct if

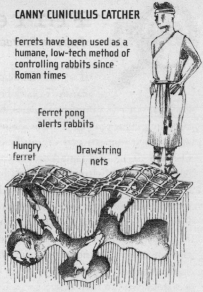

CANNY CUNICULUS CATCHER

Ferrets have been used as a humane, low-tech method of controlling rabbits since Roman times

Ferret pong alerts rabbits

Hungry ferret

Drawstring nets

they escape. Female ferrets (jills) can get sick if they aren't mated when in season. The simplest way is to keep a sterilised male (hoblet) to service them: an unfettered male (hob) might father fifteen kits a year. But be warned: ferret sex is nasty, brutish and long. The hob is much larger than the jill and has a penis shaped like a hockey stick that locks inside her for several hours, while he indulges in some fairly rough dragging and neck-biting. Rather like female cats, jill ferrets seem to need a measure of unpleasant foreplay before they release their eggs.

Ferrets also suffer from some very human ailments. Cancer of the lymphatic system and pancreas is relatively common, and they are prone to stress-related illnesses and bouts of depression, particularly if separated from a companion. Often they will refuse food, and mope for weeks. This makes them rather easier to empathise with than, say, a gerbil, and has led to their successfully deployment in 'pet therapy'. An hour spent with a ferret seems to act as positive tonic for the elderly, the depressed, and children recovering from severe illnesses.

Flea
Spring-loaded sex god

The malarial mosquito has claimed more human lives, but for Europeans at least, the horseman of the apocalypse rides a flea. None of the waves of bubonic plague that have swept Europe and Asia would have been possible without the odd personal habits of *Xenopsylla cheopis*, the Oriental rat flea. Like most of the 1,800 species included in the *Siphonaptera* order ('wingless siphons'), the rat flea is always hungry and not very fussy about where it eats. Plague starts in rodents (usually marmots) but is spread by the fleas that feed on them. Plague bacteria reproduces so quickly they block the flea's digestive passage. Very soon this produces a lot of hungry fleas, their mouthparts dripping with infected blood, ready to bite any mammal within striking distance, as more than a billion humans have found out to their cost.

Being unfussy gives fleas an advantage. Our very own species, *Pulex irritans*, has largely been banished by better hygiene but can still be found on pigs. The fleas on your dog are probably cat fleas, as they are the most common and will live on most mammals or even a passing lizard. In fact, the only consistent requirement for fleas is that an animal sleeps in a den or nest. That's because fleas' eggs aren't attached to their host. They fall off, hatch and feast on the adult fleas' droppings. This is highly efficient: as a flea sucks its way through fifteen times its own body-weight in blood a day, its other end feeds the blind wormlike larvae. Once they pupate, the cocoons can lie dormant for a year, waiting for our vibrations to hatch them.

Streamlined to move effortlessly through hair, covered in

Pet shops would be bereft without fleas: over $1 billion a year are spent on anti-flea products in the USA alone. Pliny the Elder's solution was cheaper: collect the soil under your right foot when you hear the first cuckoo of spring and sprinkle it over them.

snaggable spines and combs, fleas are hard to remove and even harder to crush. Their legendary jumping skills aren't even dependent on muscle strength. Wingless, they have turned the wing-hinge structure into a mechanical spring made from a rubbery protein called resilin. This clicks shut as the body plates compress, like a catch on a jack-in-the-box. When released, it pushes down on the leg tendons, achieving an acceleration that is fifteen times that of a space-shuttle launching. The flea uses movement-sensitive hairs to calibrate precisely the distance and direction of its jump, and pumps air into special sacs in its legs to slow down before touchdown.

Impressive as this is, the real masterpiece of flea engineering is the penis. Proportionately the longest of any insect, it has so many hooks, springs and spines that it's been compared to a Swiss army knife. Unsurprisingly, it takes a long time to unfold, but then copulation can last for three hours — the equivalent of six weeks for a human. Adult fleas are ready for this marathon as soon as they emerge. No wonder a single pair of fleas can produce another 50,000 in a month, or that Carl Djerassi, the creator of the contraceptive pill for humans, also developed one for fleas.

BUNNY LOVING

Rabbit fleas breed in sync with their host

Pregnant rabbit hormones stimulate the female fleas' ovaries to grow

Both sexes leave the doe once her young are born

Pheromones in the young rabbit's urine puts both fleas in the mood

Adults return to the doe

They mate and lay eggs

Young fleas hatch and feed on the tasty babies

Fly
Sultan of sperm

Flies are insects with two wings. Mayflies, dragonflies, fireflies and butterflies are not flies. There are 120,000 known species of true fly (almost 7,000 in the UK alone) between them carrying more than a million species of bacteria. The common housefly (*Musca domestica*) is among the most dangerous animals in the world. It breeds in rubbish, sewage and dung, and spreads tuberculosis, typhoid, cholera, dysentery, anthrax and parasitic worms by excreting, walking and vomiting on food.

Flies are prodigious breeders. In warm weather, the life-cycle from egg through maggot to adult lasts just eight to twelve days. Theoretically, two flies mating in April could produce 191,010,000,000,000,000,000 descendants by August: enough to cover the earth in a blanket of horridness 47 feet deep. But only a small proportion of flies are pests: most are essential for pollination and the recycling of decaying matter.

Flies have been much misunderstood throughout history. Arisotle confused the generations that followed him by implying flies had four legs and two 'arms', and this was repeated in academic texts for more than a thousand years as no one bothered to look at a fly and check. Only in 1688 did the Italian biologist Francesco Redi disprove what everyone also believed: that maggots spontaneously generate from meat.

Flies land on the ceiling by zooming in close, reaching up with their front legs and flipping their whole body over

> In Luoyang city in central China the local authority is buying dead flies off residents for 0.06 cents each to promote public hygiene. This is reminiscent of Mao's 1955 'four harms' campaign against flies, rats, mosquitoes and sparrows. It was stopped when the collapse in the sparrow population led to an explosion of crop-eating insects.

backwards. They walk around up there thanks to their sticky feet. These are covered in tiny hairs that produce a glue-like substance made of sugars and oils. They are also equipped with a pair of minute claws so they can detach themselves on departure.

Of the flies that are pests, among the most serious are fruit flies: every year they cause billions of dollars of losses in fruit, vegetable and flower crops. Yet they are the most studied and the most fascinating flies of all. Cheap, easy to handle and quickly anaesthetised, it is easy to tell males from females and they breed extremely fast, so that many generations can be studied in a short time. The discovery of chromosomes, which won Thomas Hunt Morgan a Nobel Prize in 1933, stemmed from his work on fruit flies. It turns out that 61 per cent of human diseases have fruit-fly equivalents. Scientists who work on fruit-fly genes (known as drosophilists) like to give appropriate names to their more unusual discoveries. Flies with the 'Groucho' gene have more face bristles than normal and 'Maggies' have arrested development, like the baby in *The Simpsons*. Flies with the 'Ken and Barbie' gene have no external genitalia. This is a rare fruit-fly indeed. While the human sperm cell is the smallest in the body –

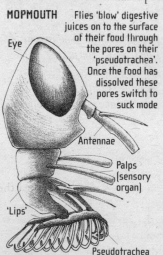

MOPMOUTH
Flies 'blow' digestive juices on to the surface of their food through the pores on their 'pseudotrachea'. Once the food has dissolved these pores switch to suck mode

Eye

Antennae

Palps (sensory organ)

'Lips'

Pseudotrachea

it's only a 500th of an inch long – and a blue whale has sperm only a 5,000th of an inch longer than that – most male fruit-flies are real men. One species has sperm that is 2.3 inches in length – the longest in nature – and its testicles make up a whopping 11 per cent of its body-weight. That's proportionately larger than our heads. Fruit flies were the first animals in space and are still used by NASA today. They've come a long way since their four-legged ancestors of the Middle Ages.

Fossa

Girl becomes boy becomes girl . . .

The fossa (*Cryptoprocta ferox*) is only found on Madagascar, where it is the top land carnivore. It's the size of a spaniel, looks like a cat, but is distantly related to the mongoose. Imagine a cross between a puma and a giant otter that leaps through the branches like a squirrel and you're close. Its name is a Malagasy word, pronounced 'FOO-sa'.

Among many odd things about fossa, one remains completely unexplained and unique. The young females start to grow a penis. Actually, it's a big clitoris, but it has a bone in it and is covered in the same vicious looking backward-facing spines as the male appendage. They leak the bright orange discharge of a sexually mature adult male and develop genital bumps that look like testes. Odder still, when they reach maturity at four years old, all this stops and the clitoris shrinks back to normal size.

Quite why the young fossa females want to look like males baffles zoologists. It isn't accompanied by a surge in male hormones, or aggression, as in hyenas. Maybe it's just to keep the boys away until they are ready to mate.

A brief examination of their mating habits tends to confirm this. A female in heat will climb to the top of a tree, while at its

THE DOG-CAT-MONGOOSE THAT LIVES IN A TREE

Canine nostril pad

Feline long whiskers for night hunting

Canine/feline long sharp teeth

Feline retractable claws

Walks on soles like mongoose – or on tip toes like cats and dogs

Anal scent glands like mongoose

Feline 3-foot tail for balance

foot a pack of males gather, making threatening calls and getting into ferocious fights. The female will mate with several males over the course of a week, before another female climbs the tree to take her place. Each copulation lasts up to three hours, punctuated by licking, biting and yowling as they somehow manage to stay in the branches. The spiny male penis locks them rear to rear, like dogs.

> *The fossa's Latin name, Cryptoprocta ferox, means 'ferocious hidden anus' – because a pouch covers the anus and contains glands that it uses to mark its territory.*

Fossa were first described in 1833, but haven't been studied in depth until recently. Madagascar – which is three times the size of the British Isles – separated from the mainland of Africa over 165 million years ago and four-fifths of its plants and animals are found there and nowhere else.

Genetic evidence suggests that the eight Malagasy carnivores are all descended from a single species of mongoose that 'blew in' from African thirty million years ago. That makes fossa a direct relative of the common ancestor of cats and dogs, which is certainly how they look.

They are ferocious hunters, and although they don't actually attack cattle they will take on large female lemurs, consuming everything: fur, bones, and claws. They will also kill snakes, rodents, fish and birds. Their biggest threat, predictably, is the human destruction of their environment. Since their arrival a mere 1,500 years ago, humans have cleared 95 per cent of the forests that covered the island.

Madagascan people have a deep fear of fossa, partly owing to the folk memories of a recently extinct fossa relative which was the size of a tiger. Malagasy parents scare their children with tales of them stealing babies, or killing all the chickens in a coop with their terrible flatulence.

Zoologists estimate there are 2,500 fossa left, but can't be certain. They are masters of concealment: some researchers who have studied lemurs for years have never seen a fossa.

Fox
Clever not cruel

The red fox (*Vulpes vulpes*) is easily the most widespread and abundant wild carnivore on earth. Foxes are astonishingly adaptable and are found almost everywhere in the world, from deserts to the Arctic Circle. But unlike many of its close relatives, including the wolf, the fox is in no danger of being persecuted out of existence: it is the ultimate opportunist and has learnt to live alongside humans, without sacrificing any of its feral integrity.

Despite this, the number of urban foxes isn't increasing 'exponentially'; in most Western cities the population reached its maximum supportable size years ago, and the count of surviving cubs each year is almost identical to the number of deaths. The fox population explosion, like almost everything people think they know about urban foxes, is an urban myth. Even the term itself is inaccurate: 'urban' foxes are mostly sub-urban – they don't like city centres but prefer areas of low-density, semi-detached housing with big gardens, which is why Britain has so many (North American suburbs have raccoons instead).

> In Japan, foxes are sacred to the Shinto religion and 'fox possession' is a recognised clinical condition. Symptoms include a craving for rice and an inability to make eye contact.

Urban foxes are just as healthy as country foxes; the town is, if anything, a better environment for them than the countryside. They don't live 'mainly' by scavenging from bins. Foxes will eat literally almost anything: it's what makes them so successful. Their regular diet includes earthworms, insects, moth larvae, pigeons, rodents, beetles and plenty of fruit and veg. In the autumn, they can practically live on apples, blackberries and rosehips.

They don't 'hunt in packs' or kill cats. Foxes live in small family groups, but always hunt alone. They would never attack a domestic cat or dog unless cornered (although they've been known to try their luck with swans). Nor do they massacre chickens 'for fun'. Foxes are cache-hunters: they will take as many animals as they can, and then bury the carcasses one by one in a 'larder' for later. The reason they leave dead chickens behind in the coop is that they are disturbed on one of their many trips to and from the larder.

Most of the nuisance caused by foxes is far outweighed by their indispensable role as rodent-killers. Even the deeply annoying habit of digging up lawns and sports fields is not entirely their fault, as they mistake the smell of blood and-bone fertiliser on the grass for dead meat, and try to uncover a non-existent corpse. On the other hand, don't encourage them to nest under your house. At night, the noise of the cubs screaming as they fight and play is indescribable, almost as bad as the smell of carrion, urine and faeces (the latter will be cheerfully deposited as a 'mark' on any shoes or children's toys you leave outside). They also enjoy chewing through electricity and phone wires, and gas and water pipes.

Urban foxes can easily become tame, even allowing themselves to be fed from the hand and stroked like a pet. This latent tameness was selectively bred in a famous Russian experiment of the 1950s. Within twenty years, the foxes had lost all fear of humans, wagged their tails, developed floppy ears and black and white fur: they had become, in effect, 'dogs'.

MOUSE DIVING

1. Fox leaps

2. Descends vertically

3 feet

Foxes are better at catching mice than cats

3. Startled mouse leaps upwards (big mistake)

Frog
Toxic paradox

In fairy-tales, frogs are ugly but kind; in real life, they are breathtakingly lovely and deadly dangerous. Such is true, at least, of the brilliantly coloured tree frogs of South America. Their neon reds, shocking oranges, acid greens, purples and blues cover the entire visible spectrum and their eyes are like precious stones.

The world's deadliest frog is the Golden poison dart frog, *Phyllobates terribilis*. Sometimes mint-green, sometimes Kodak yellow, it is no larger than a bottle-top but contains enough toxins to kill 20,000 mice or ten men. An amount of its poison weighing less than three grains of salt is sufficient to kill a person and even just to hold one in your hand can be lethal. Poison dart frogs are so called because tribesmen use their venom to tip the missiles of their blowpipes. Captain James Cochrane first discovered this in 1823. He also found out how they extracted the poison: skewering the frog so painfully that it sweated it out. The second most poisonous frog in the world is the Black-legged dart frog (*Phyllobates bicolor*) of Colombia. It is bright orange or yellow with navy-blue legs. The locals make this one sweat by heating it over a flame.

> To vomit, some frog species cough up their whole stomach and then carefully rinse it out with their right hand before pushing it back inside.

As a general rule, the more beautiful the frog, the more dangerous it is. This is called aposematism, from the Greek for 'warning sign'. The tiny, red-and-white-striped Ecuadorean tree frog, *Epipedobates tricolor,* seems to be wearing a Sunderland FC strip or impersonating a barber's pole. Comical? Certainly not: it will kill you. Other species aren't dangerous but have evolved to look as if they are. The Red-eyed tree frog of Costa Rica is green with blue-and-yellow striped sides, orange toes and liquid scarlet

FROGGY GOES A-COURTIN'

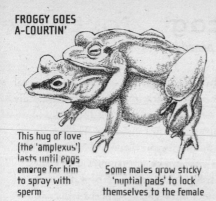

This hug of love (the 'amplexus') lasts until eggs emerge for him to spray with sperm

Some males grow sticky 'nuptial pads' to lock themselves to the female

eyes. It has a call that sounds like a baby rattle-snake but it is com-pletely harmless. This is called Batesian mimicry after Henry Walter Bates (1825–92) who spent seven years in the Amazon with Alfred Russell Wallace and found 8,000 creatures new to science.

Trinidad's Paradoxical frog (*Pseudis paradoxa*) is so called because its tadpoles are three times larger than the adult, but frogs and paradoxes go hand in hand. There are over 5,000 known species and new ones turn up all the time – a hundred in Sri Lanka in 2002 alone. But they're also dying out at an alarming rate: a third of all frogs are at risk, because frogs breathe through their skin. Though their toxins can occasionally be dangerous to us, the poisons that humans leave lying around are far deadlier to them. This may be a tragedy for both of us. Frog toxins are alkaloids – like cocaine, nicotine, codeine, caffeine and quinine – and scientists are finding that these beautiful paradoxes are living medicine chests, whose deadly poisons can be transformed into drugs that

Occasionally a lustful male will attach himself to an old boot or dead fish by mistake

may cure everything from cancer to Alzheimer's disease. *Epipedobates tricolor* yields a painkiller 200 times more powerful than morphine; *Phyllobates terribilis* provides another 600 times as powerful. Both are non-addictive, with no side effects. Inside other frogs may be muscle relaxants and heart stimulants, and cures for strokes, bacterial infections and depression. There is a prince in there, after all.

Giant Tortoise
Large slow larder

In 2006, Adwaitya, the Aldabra giant tortoise (*Geochelone gigantes*), personal pet of Clive of India, died in Kolkata zoo, aged 255. He was, as far as we know, the planet's oldest animal inhabitant and it is astonishing to imagine a life that began before Mozart and the French Revolution ending with an announcement on CNN. Tortoise longevity is driven by a slow reproductive hit rate. Giant tortoises are big, cold-blooded herbivores, with a sluggish metabolism. It takes them at least thirty years to reach sexual maturity and although, as adults, they have few natural predators, their young are not so lucky. Even the isolation of an island is no protection: only one egg in ten makes it to adolescence. So, a long life means a much better chance of passing on the genes.

The origins of giant tortoises stretch back fifty million years, to the time when the first turtles hauled themselves on to the land. They were able to exploit the niches left behind by large plant-eating dinosaurs and, predictably, started to grow large. One giant tortoise, *Colossochelys atlas*, was the size of a small car and spread across the globe, even colonising Antarctica. But the combination of a cooling climate and human ingenuity condemned them (the shell is an effective barrier to teeth and claws, but becomes an all-in-one cooking pot on a fire). By 1750, when Adwaitya emerged blinking from his shell, there were no continental giant tortoises left, but 250 species basking happily on their predator-free

TORTOISE DINGHY

Despite weighing 40 stone, giant tortoises are good swimmers

They can drift for up to 500 miles

islands. Today, there are only twelve species, all but one of them endangered.

Giant tortoises' heads gradually grew too big to be withdrawn into their shells – they had survived for so long without attack that even this protection deserted them. They also suffered the misfortune of tasting delicious. Although Darwin – whose

> Giant tortoise oil was considered so delicious that it was the only way of making the flesh of the dodo – called the 'disgusting bird' by the Dutch – palatable.

theories of natural selection owed so much to the Galápagos species – thought them 'indifferent' eating, most early accounts were ecstatic. One giant tortoise would feed several men, and both its meat and its fat were perfectly digestible, the liver was a peerless feast and the bones were rich with gorgeous marrow. Then there were the eggs: the best eggs anyone had ever eaten. Even more useful to sailors, the tortoises could be taken alive on board ship and survive for at least six months without food or water. Stacked helplessly on their backs, they could be killed and eaten as and when necessary. Better still, because they sucked up gallons of water at a time and kept it in a special bladder, a carefully butchered tortoise was also a fountain of cool, perfectly drinkable water.

Unsurprisingly, it took 300 years after its first discovery for the giant tortoise to receive a scientific name: the specimens were all eaten before they got back to the scientists. Worse still, large-scale commercial whaling in the nineteenth century was only made possible because the giant tortoises enabled ships to stay at sea for weeks at a time. One ship's log records 'turpining' parties taking 14 tons of live tortoises on board one ship in four days.

If there is a glimmer of hope it concerns Adwaitya's descendants. In 1875, the government of Mauritius, inspired by Albert Gunter of the British Museum, declared *Geochelone gigantes* the world's first protected species. There are now 152,000 Aldabras – 90 per cent of the world's total giant tortoise population – happily isolated from their only serious threat: us.

Gibbon
The talking ape

One of the odd things about the great apes — our closest primate relatives like the chimpanzee and the gorilla — is that their vocal communication is relatively unsophisticated compared to our own.

Not so the thirteen species of gibbons that live in the tropical forests of South-East Asia. Gibbons aren't monkeys — they don't have tails or cheek pouches — but 'lesser apes', and their calls are some of the most beautiful and idiosyncratic sounds made by any animal. Gibbons use these calls to communicate precise messages, assembling elements of each call into a string which has a meaning that is understood by other gibbons in their family group, who use a similar sequence in return. Linguists call this 'syntax' — the linking of sounds in a particular way to create meaning — and it is the basis of all language.

The development of this language may be linked to the fact that gibbons — unlike most other monkeys and apes — are monogamous. Like songbirds, gibbons sing to attract and keep a mate and to mark their territory, particularly their favourite fruit trees. To snag the best female to breed with, a male gibbon has to work on his singing. For females, the better the singer, the better the genes, and the more regular the supply of fruit.

Couples sing to each other every morning in fabulously complex duets. Males sing before dawn, sometimes

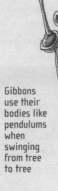

KING OF THE SWINGERS

'Multiflex' wrists

Gibbons use their bodies like pendulums when swinging from tree to tree while still in 'bed', which for a gibbon means sitting high up in the branches, with their arms hugging their knees and their heads tucked into their laps. Females are much more active and dramatic, breaking branches, leaping and climaxing with a sequence called the 'great call'. Males who have a mate sing more

> No one knows how the gibbon got its name. The French naturalist Buffon coined it, maybe as a version of 'gibb', the old name for cat, or in honour of his friend Edward Gibbon, the historian.

regularly when there are rogue males sniffing around, as you'd expect.

Most family groups comprise a male and female living with three or four offspring, some of whom don't leave home until they are ten years old. Because of their energy-poor diet – fruit, leaves, and the occasional insect – families spend half their time just hanging around grooming one another. The female rules the roost at home; the males are right at the bottom of the hierarchy, even below the offspring. In some species the male takes over childcare once the young are weaned, teaching them how to swing.

Gibbons are built to swing. Their arms are longer than their legs and bodies combined, and strong enough to propel them at speeds of 35 mph and across 50-foot gaps between trees. Their wrist bones are separated by soft pads which allow movement in all directions. This enables them to swing and change direction without having to turn their bodies – saving energy and giving them the breathtaking agility for which they're best known. On the rare occasions they walk on the ground, gibbons are bipedal, which has led researchers to propose that walking on two feet might originally have developed as an unforeseen by-product of arm-swinging in the canopy.

In Thai mythology, gibbons are the reincarnated souls of lost lovers. In one story, a woman searching for her murdered husband wanders the forests to this day repeating the gibbon's plaintive song, 'Pau! Pau!' (Thai for 'husband').

Giraffe
Big head, bad smell

The ability to reach the leaves at the very top of trees seems reason enough to grow a long neck, but a giraffe's neck is about more than just food. Male giraffes use their necks as weapons and as signs of their virility. There's nothing cute about 'necking' between male giraffes; they lock them together like arm-wrestlers or swing their heads like medieval maces, with a terrifying force that can topple or kill their opponents with a single blow (a giraffe's skull weighs more than a full-size boxer's punchbag and sports up to five skin-covered horns called *ossicones*). Unlike the female's, the male giraffe's neck and skull continue to grow thicker throughout its life. The bigger the neck, the more victories, and the greater number of willing females that come flocking. To counter-balance the weight of these heavy-duty sex toys, the giraffe's neck has evolved with one more vertebra than other mammals, at the point where it joins the chest.

The other key weapon in a male giraffe's lady-killing armoury is his odour: downwind you can

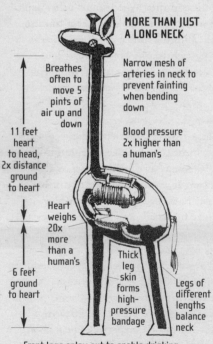

MORE THAN JUST A LONG NECK

Breathes often to move 5 pints of air up and down

Narrow mesh of arteries in neck to prevent fainting when bending down

Blood pressure 2x higher than a human's

11 feet heart to head, 2x distance ground to heart

6 feet ground to heart

Heart weighs 20x more than a human's

Thick leg skin forms high-pressure bandage

Legs of different lengths balance neck

Front legs splay out to enable drinking

smell one from over 800 feet away. Early explorers compared their scent to 'a hive of heather honey in September', but the key chemical constituent is indole, the nitrogen compound that gives our faeces their characteristic smell. As well as driving females wild, giraffe-pong has a practical function, acting as an inbuilt parasite repellent and killing many of the microbes and fungal organisms that graze on a giraffe's skin. Giraffes even secrete the active ingredient in creosote to kill bloodsucking ticks. As far as they are concerned, smelling bad means you are clean and healthy.

> The Romans exhibited giraffes in their amphitheatres as 'camelopards', assuming they were a cross between camels and leopards.

Most of a giraffe's life is spent either eating or chewing the cud. Their favourite meal is the acacia tree, which is so thorny that most other animals leave it alone. The top joint of their neck allows them to raise their heads vertically in line with the neck and browse for the young thornless leaves at the very top. Amazingly, the trees have learned to fight back by releasing a chemical that turns their leaves bitter. They also release a wind-borne 'warning burst' to alert surrounding trees to do the same. Giraffes, in turn, always try to approach acacias upwind.

Next to the neck, the other essential device is the tongue, which can extend up to 20 inches, long enough to clean their ears. A grasping tool with the same level of dexterity as three human fingers, a giraffe's tongue is used so often that it has taken on a blue-black colour to reduce the risk of sunburn.

Giraffes need less water than camels, and as acacia leaves are 70 per cent water, they rarely need to drink. This is good news, because their awkward splayed pose at a waterhole leaves them vulnerable to lions and crocodiles. The only time they kneel is to sleep, laying their head on the ground for ten minutes each day and, even then, keeping half their brain awake.

Giraffes are often hunted for their tail tuft which, at over 3 feet, is among the longest hair found on any mammal. It is used for bracelets and as an unofficial currency in Sudan and Uganda.

Goat
The farmer's friend

Far from being a poor relation of sheep and cattle, the goat (*Capra hircus*) was the first herbivore to be domesticated, 10,000 years ago in the mountains of Iran. Without goats, agriculture might never have taken off. The bezoar or wild goat (*Capra aegagrus*), ancestor of all domestic breeds, seduced the Neolithic nomads with its hardiness, its 'herdability', and its weed-busting diet. Goats, then as now, much prefer thistles, brambles and twigs to plain grass (a grass-fed goat suffers badly from worms). It was an unbeatable combination and as the first farmers radiated outwards from the Middle East, the goats followed as a kind of all-terrain convenience store, every bit as revolutionary in their time as seed-drills or combine-harvesters.

In developing countries, goats are still a very important economic resource. They produce more milk for their size than cows and some estimates put goat ahead of chicken and pork as the world's most consumed meat. Even in the US, goat is now the fastest-growing livestock sector. The meat is healthy, with much less fat and cholesterol and more iron than lamb

> The word 'tragedy' comes from ancient Greek and means 'goat-song'.

or beef. Goat's milk has more protein and calcium, and less lactose than cow's milk. They also make good pets, and are surprisingly fastidious. If another goat's saliva has touched their food, or if it has even the faintest taint of dirt, they will refuse to eat it.

The only downside is the smell. 'Goatiness' comes from a trio of fatty acids present in both the milk and the meat. These are also produced as waste products by the ten million or so bacteria that feed in the human armpit, which might explain our squeamishness. Female goats on heat, however, find it irresistible.

Goats have a reputation for lust and excess which has a sound basis in fact. A male goat (buck or billy) is ready for action at just four months. As he comes into 'rut', he begins to smell strongly – this is not helped by a fondness for urinating along his belly and soaking his beard. To really get in the mood, he will lick his penis and then drink the urine of his prospective partners. The nannies (or does) either stand back and watch until they are needed, or mount one another to further inflame his ardour.

> In Sudan in 2006, a man caught having sex with his neighbour's goat was forced to marry it and pay a dowry to its former owner.

The man–goat relationship can be equally close. Alexander Selkirk, the castaway who was the real-life model for *Robinson Crusoe*, used to mark the ears of the goats he 'enjoyed most' so as to avoid eating them. The ancient Gauls made goat's milk haircream. For a thousand years, the sum of human knowledge was recorded on goatskin parchment. Young goat's leather made soft gloves (hence the expression 'handle with kid gloves') and the hair from their backs gave us cashmere, the fashionable yarn for ladies; its name is an old spelling of Kashmir, the region where the longhaired goats come from. In 2002 a herd of Canadian goats was implanted with a single spider gene. When their milk was skimmed and the protein extracted it made a fibre that was identical to spider silk. It has been patented as BioSteel.

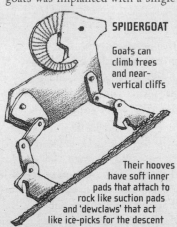

SPIDERGOAT

Goats can climb trees and near-vertical cliffs

Their hooves have soft inner pads that attach to rock like suction pads and 'dewclaws' that act like ice-picks for the descent

Goats have a much greater mythological resonance than sheep or cattle. The horn of plenty belonged to a goat. Pan and Satan had goat's legs and horns, and in Hindu mythology *aja* means both 'goat' and the primordial nothingness from which everything came.

Goose
Smart and saucy

Despite having acquired a reputation for stupidity, geese show signs of great sensitivity and intelligence. Many species mate for life and the death of a loved one leads to behaviour that is remarkably similar to our own. They honk mournfully, stop eating, hunch up their feathers and can remain that way for months. If one is shot down, its partner will return to earth to stand vigil next to its corpse. Reunited couples perform a 'triumph ceremony' – a combination of dance and song which re-enacts their courtship. Geese can even be taught to perform simple tasks – there are several nineteenth-century accounts of them turning spits, using their powerful necks like an arm.

The French ornithologist Christian Moullec has taught a group of thirty endangered Lesser white-fronted Geese (*Anser erythropus*) a new migratory path. After bonding with them as goslings, he flew a microlight to lead them the 1,000 miles between wildlife sanctuaries in Germany and Sweden, a journey they repeated the following year on their own. They are now so well trained that Moullec and his 'flock' regularly appear as the star turn at airshows.

Although farmyard geese rarely fly, the wild birds are amazing long-distance aviators. Six million Lesser snow geese (*Chen caerulescens caerulescens*) travel the 4,000 miles from the Arctic to the Gulf of Mexico twice a year. The

THE CHIMNEY SWEEP'S GOOSE

Rope tied round neck and goose pushed down chimney

Complaining goose dislodges tar and soot

Barheaded goose (*Anser indicus*) migrates from Central Asia to India over the Himalayas at a height of 29,000 feet. The swirl of air created by flying in V-formation produces more lift and a clearer view for each bird. They lose altitude by whiffling – a spiralling nosedive, which sometimes leaves them flying upside down.

People wrote with goose quills until the nineteenth century. 'Pen' comes from the latin 'penna', or 'feather'. Quink, the world's top selling ink, is also an old name for the Brent goose.

Geese were domesticated about 3,000 years ago in ancient Egypt from the wild Greylag goose (*lag* is an old word for 'goose', so we should really just call them greylags). It had more to do with sex than food. Wild greylags were the focus of fertility cults throughout the ancient world and goose fat was considered a powerful aphrodisiac. The famous geese on the Capitoline Hill, who saved Rome from the Gauls in 390 BC, were being kept as sexual talismans not 'guard dogs'.

The connection is still alive in the innuendo of the nursery rhyme 'Goosey, goosey, gander' and for centuries *goose* was slang for a prostitute while *gooser* meant penis. The verb 'to goose' still carries a sexual connotation.

Because no one ever saw a migratory goose mate or lay an egg, for centuries it was thought they hatched from the barnacles washed ashore on driftwood at the same time of year as they arrived from the Arctic. This belief persisted well into the days when scientists were naming species; thus today we have the Barnacle goose (*Branta leucopsis*) and the Goose barnacle (*Lepas anatifera*).

It caused confusion for the Catholic Church, too. Some dioceses allowed the eating of geese on fast days because they were 'fish', others because they were 'not born of the flesh', and therefore a kind of vegetable or nut. Pope Innocent III finally banned goose-eating on fast days in 1215.

Gorilla
Going ape

Gorillas are the largest living primates and the most misunderstood. Their name dates to 480 BC when the Carthaginian explorer Hanno described an African tribe of 'hairy women'. He called them *Gorillai* and it was this that American missionary Dr Thomas Savage decided to use to describe the 'monkey-like animal remarkable for its size and ferocity' whose skull he'd seen when he visited the Congo in 1847. In the popular imagination, Savage's gorilla came to personify animals at their most wild and terrifying, a myth that culminated in the 1933 film *King Kong*.

Real gorillas are shy and peaceful creatures. They are herbivores, eating green plants and bark. To run a 25-stone male gorilla requires a straw bale's weight in vegetation every day, which is why they have such huge stomachs (to house the large intestinal tract) and heads (to anchor the huge jaw muscles needed for chewing). It also explains their habit of eating their own droppings; as with rabbits, this helps them extract the maximum nutrition and re-cycle helpful digestive bacteria and enzymes. Also, because leafy plants are low in sodium, gorillas supplement their green diet with tasty mouthfuls of soil.

Both species of Gorilla, western (*G. gorilla*) and eastern (*G. beringei*), live in the equatorial forests of Africa where vegetation is both plentiful and fast growing. This enables them to maintain much smaller ranges than their cousins, the fruit-seeking chimps. The consequence of this is a 'harem' system where a dominant 'silverback' male lives with up to ten females and youngsters. All a single lady gorilla wants is a large, powerful male with a good-quality home range. As a result, silverbacks are much bigger than the females, but sex isn't at such a premium as among the promiscuous chimps – a silverback's erect penis is only an inch and a half long. He doesn't need to compete sexually once he's got his troop: they do what he says. At least they do until a younger male chances his arm. This is where the 'scary ape' routine derives from: standing tall, drumming chests with cupped hands, yawning to display canine teeth, roaring and charging. Actual fighting is rare; as with humans, loud threats backed up by size usually carry the day.

Despite this, gorillas are the strong, silent members of the ape family. They aren't as vocal or as flashy with their skills as chimps, but they have better memories and often do things independently rather than simply for a reward. Koko, a female gorilla born at San Francisco Zoo in 1971, has mastered up to a thousand words in sign language, and seems able to communicate complex emotions like sadness and even make jokes. She describes herself, touchingly, as 'fine animal person gorilla'.

> *The Beast was a tough guy too. He could lick the world. But when he saw Beauty, she got him. He went soft. He forgot his wisdom and the little fellas licked him.*
>
> KING KONG

It's hard to know how much of Koko's 'personhood' derives from the thirty years she has spent being coached (and loved) by developmental psychologist Dr Penny Patterson. Ironically, it was just this ability to bond with a human that spelt doom for Kong in the film. Given the precarious position of the gorilla population (10,000 western gorillas and only 400 of the mountain species), maybe Koko's willingness to learn and talk in our language, will persuade us to rewrite *King Kong*'s tragic ending and preserve her relatives in the wild, where they are happiest.

FORWARD PLANNING

Gorillas have only recently been observed to use tools – stones as hammers, leaves as napkins and sticks to gauge the depth of ponds

Hedgehog
Disappearing lawn urchin

Snuffling in the dark and gorging on insects, the hedgehog hasn't changed much in fifteen million years. But, in spite of regularly topping the polls as the UK's favourite garden animal, the British hedgehog population is now in freefall. It has halved in the past fifteen years and the current estimate is below a million. If this continues there will be no British hedgehogs left by 2030.

Half die before they reach their first birthday; only 1 in 100 makes it to five, and 15,000 are squashed on British roads each year (down from the mid-1990s peak of 100,000). Road carnage combined with the use of powerful insecticides and the destruction of the grassy field margins that hedgehogs like to nest in make it hard to feel optimistic. Even 'urban hedgehogs' aren't as adept at surviving in cities as foxes. They fall into swimming pools, get puréed by lawnmowers or wedge their heads into food containers and starve to death (McDonalds have now changed the design of their McFlurry cartons to make them hedgehog-proof). Many also die from diarrhoea caused by well meaning humans leaving them bread and milk. The best way to help a hedgehog is not to feed it but to turn it loose in your vegetable patch. A single adult can eat 250 slugs in an evening.

> The fox knows many things; the hedgehog, one big thing.
>
> ERASMUS

Ironically, because of their 'spiny ball' defence, hedgehogs have very few natural predators. Badgers are the only animals with claws strong enough to prise open a rolled hedgehog, although hungry foxes have been known to urinate on them to force them to unroll. Hedgehogs also have an extraordinary immunity to poison. It takes more chloroform to put a hedgehog to sleep than any other animal of comparable size and they can survive a bite from an adder that would kill a guinea pig in five minutes.

This resistance offers a clue to the strangest of all hedgehog behaviours: 'self-anointing', which involves them contorting themselves to coat their own back with gobbets of foaming saliva. Hedgehogs have been observed self-anointing after chewing on the poisonous skin of a toad, thereby creating a toxic mousse for their spines. This makes them even less attractive to predators, but it doesn't entirely explain why the smell of shoes, cigar butts, furniture polish, creosote, coffee, boiled fish, face cream and distilled water should also stimulate the same behaviour.

Spines act as shock absorbers – a rolled-up hedgehog can bounce down a flight of steps without any difficulty

The word *heyghoge* is first recorded in 1450 and this quickly splintered into regional nicknames like highoggs, hedgepigs, hoghogs and fuzzipeggs. Before that, the Anglo-Saxons had called them *igl* and the Normans, 'urchins', after the Latin for hedgehog, *ericius*. This came from the ancient root *gher-*, meaning 'to bristle' (which also gave us 'horror').

An adult hedgehog bristles with over 5,000 spines. They are hollow hairs, reinforced by keratin, the same substance our nails are made from. They are extremely strong; a hedgehog can be picked up by a single spine without it breaking. Considering the physical barrier, hedgehogs of both sexes are remarkably promiscuous, mating with ten or more partners each season and sometimes several on the same night. It is never face-to-face, despite Aristotle's confident assertions. The male circles a female for hours, snorting loudly until she spreads her back legs, flattens her spikes and points her nose upwards. Copulation is very brief and noisy and, once sated, the male immediately trundles off, taking no further interest in the female or the rearing of his offspring.

Hoatzin
Half-bird, half-cow

Very few birds live by munching on vegetation. It's heavy, low in energy and slow to digest, not the ideal fuel for flying. But the strange hoatzin (*Opisthocomus hoazin*) – pronounced 'watseen' – of the South American river swamps has actually developed a stomach like a cow's to cope with its diet of leaves.

Crop reduces space for flight muscles, making hoatzins bad flyers

They prefer to scrabble around in the branches

The hoatzin's crop is enormous, fifty times larger than its stomach, accounting for almost a third of total body-weight. And unlike most birds, where it is used for storage, the hoatzin's crop does most of the digestive heavy work. Like the foregut of a cow, it is full of bacteria and enzymes which break down the cellulose in the leaves. An amazing 70 per cent of the fibre gets digested, but as with cows, this takes time. Hoatzins take two days to digest a meal, the slowest of any bird.

The downside of eating like a cow is smelling like one, which is why the hoatzin is known as the 'stink bird'. The manure-like pong is produced by fermenting fatty acids in the crop and has kept them mostly out of the human food chain, although their eggs are eaten. The intrepid American ornithologist William Beebe cooked and ate a hoatzin in 1909 and declared it 'clean and appetising'. More recently, microbiologists have studied the crop bacteria because of its ability to neutralise poisons in the toxic foliage the bird eats. Transferred to cows and goats, these might allow them to graze on a wider range of forage, with an enormous increase in yield.

They are very social birds, living in groups of five to fifty, and are about as large (and clumsy) as chickens. Their weight makes them poor flyers and they spend three-quarters of their time just perching, spreading their feathers to soak up the sun and digesting their toxic breakfast. They look rather prehistoric, with shaggy russet and light brown feathers, a bright blue face, piercing red eyes with large eyelashes and a spiky head crest. They are noisy, too: continually grunting, wheezing, and hissing.

What is a hoatzin? Taxonomists still can't agree. Even with genetic analysis they don't quite fit into any of the existing bird families. For a long time they were classed as game birds (*uazin* is the Aztec name for pheasant), then as cuckoos and more recently as doves. Now, most reference sources list them, aardvark-like, as a single species in their own order, the Opisthocomiformes – 'ones with long hair behind', referring to their large crest.

Their chicks share a feature with the fossil proto-bird, archaeopteryx: the first two 'fingers' of the wing form into two claws. If disturbed, chicks as young as three days old will leap into the water, and clamber back through the branches to the nest using their claws like small monkeys. It's unlikely that the claws are a prehistoric survival; they are just another odd adaptation to life in the swamp, and disappear as the birds grow older.

A BUMPER CROP

'How do you keep from falling off?'

'Alimentary, my dear hoatzin.'

To balance, the hoatzin has a leathery bump on the bottom of its crop, which it rests on a branch while perching

Horse
Made in America

The horse, like the dog and the camel, first carved out its evolutionary niche in the North America of 50 million years ago. In those days, it scampered around the rainforest eating fruit, much as its relative the tapir still does today. But as the planet cooled, and the forests were replaced by vast grass-filled plains, the American proto-horses diversified and adapted themselves to the new environment, eventually crossing the Bering land-bridge into Asia. All our breeds of domestic horse are a single species, *Equus caballus*, descended from these American immigrants; only one wild horse, the Mongolian Przewalski's horse (*Equus ferus przewalskii*) has survived.

Horses are animals of the steppe, and many of the adaptations that allowed them to thrive in an open landscape of rough grass continue to affect their behaviour today. Poor diet requires a large digestive tract, so they grew larger. Because they aren't ruminants,

Many cultures still eat horse, especially Kazakhs, who even eat horse rectum, and the French, whose preference allegedly dates to the Battle of Eylau in 1807, when Napoleon's surgeon-in-chief advised the starving troops to eat dead battlefield horses.

horses depend on lots of small meals, to maintain energy levels, rather than one large feast. They are 'hind-gut fermenters', absorbing nutrients through their intestines rather than their stomachs, so a change in diet can cause serious problems: over-rich pasture, mouldy hay and unfamiliar or toxic plants can cause colic, or even death. Horses are prey animals: the best defence on the steppe is to run faster than your predator. Hence they have the largest eyes of any land mammal, arranged to give them almost 360° vision. Anything unfamiliar (like a plastic bag) triggers the flight response. Also, because endurance is more important to survival than initial speed, horses' legs became longer and more powerful, but took time and space to reach top speed. Most humans can beat a horse from a standing start over 50 yards.

This might explain why most of our early interaction with horses seems to involve us killing them for meat. The oldest European hominid fossil, 500,000-year-old Boxgrove Man, was found next to a butchered horse. In their original homeland of North America, the native horse was hunted to extinction by the end of the last ice age. It wasn't until Cortez and his Spanish troops arrived in 1492 that Native Americans met their first modern horse. They called them 'big dogs', quite reasonably, as they had relied on dogs for transport until then.

No one can quite agree when we first started riding horses as well as eating them. They were probably domesticated independently many times and in many places, but the earliest known evidence points to the Ukraine around 6,000 years ago, which is several hundred years before the oldest known wheel. It was one of the great breakthroughs in human history (and an evolutionary meal ticket for the horse). Suddenly, we could travel huge distances quickly and wage wars of unprecedented scale and savagery.

As well as being useful and nutritious, horses acquired huge symbolic value, and were worshipped all over the ancient world from China and Mongolia to ancient Egypt and Celtic Europe. Their importance in this regard has never waned, even as their role in combat, agriculture and transport has diminished. In the UK and US alone, there are 10 million horses ridden for pleasure and profit, creating an income in excess of £60 billion, a figure which outstrips the gross domestic product of most of the world's poorest nations.

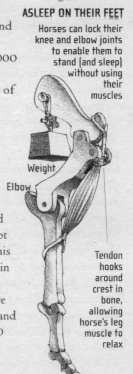

ASLEEP ON THEIR FEET

Horses can lock their knee and elbow joints to enable them to stand (and sleep) without using their muscles

Weight

Elbow

Tendon hooks around crest in bone, allowing horse's leg muscle to relax

Human
The storytelling ape

What Darwin suspected, our DNA has confirmed: we are remarkably similar to our primate cousins – we share about 97 per cent with gorillas, and over 98 per cent with chimps, although the developmental difference those very particular genes makes is clearly evident. (Interestingly we are 'hairier' than chimps, having more follicles, but their hair is thicker and longer.) The physiological differences are small: our hands are able to make two grips that a chimp can't; from this one modification all our manual dexterity has flowed. Combined with a gradual preference for walking on our hind legs (which still causes us physical difficulties), it's not impossible to see how freeing our hands also freed our minds. There is strong evidence pointing to language – the greatest of all tools – having evolved as gesture before it became speech. Culture started with our hands as well as our brains.

Why did it take us so long after we had grown our large brains and smart hands to start daubing walls, carving objects and telling stories? No one knows for sure what caused the so-called 'great leap forward' but the astonishing homogeneity of *Homo sapiens*'s DNA suggests that humans went through an ice-age 'bottleneck' around 70,000 years ago, with our population being reduced to a few thousand individuals. Life must have been tough for a long time but gradually as these pockets of humans interacted and grew larger, social relationships would have developed, tasks would have been shared and campfires lit. Among monkeys and primates, a larger social group leads to greater intelligence. Imitation, communication, learning, problem-solving are all products of primate social interactions. Among humans, it

> Human beings, who are unique in having the ability to learn from the experience of others, are also remarkable for their apparent disinclination to do so.
> DOUGLAS ADAMS

WHERE ALL THE TROUBLE STARTED

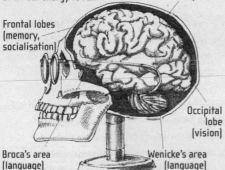

The human brain is a third larger than a chimpanzee's. It consumes 25 per cent of all our energy to run

Frontal lobes (memory, socialisation)

Parietal lobe (tool manipulation)

Occipital lobe (vision)

Broca's area (language)

Wenicke's area (language)

seems reasonable to suggest that these interactions selected for language. It's a self-reinforcing cycle: once it starts, it snowballs.

And where has the great leap taken us? We have jumped free of evolution. If we were to live in tune with the distribution curves that apply to other species, our total population would be fewer than a million. If we used primates as a guide, our communities would each be 150 individuals: large enough for breeding, small enough for there to be there are no strangers, with little crime or cheating.

But we human primates have used our brains and hands to transform the world, before our DNA could change us. We have swapped biology for history, nature for technology. The fact that you're reading this book is singularly extraordinary. You have learned a complex language, and can interpret meaning in its written form. But now this very ingenuity is creating its own limits. The animals and plants we have domesticated are so lacking in genetic diversity they are falling prey to new diseases. Globalisation means that at any one time half a million people are in the air, and millions more are on the move, their bodies and suitcases full of organisms hungry for fresh habitats. Cities – our greatest invention – are choking the planet's skies and threatening the delicate balance of climate which makes life possible.

All human cultures tell the same stories – of the man punished for stealing fire; of the flood that sweeps away all we have built. Only stories, and the imagination that feeds them, may be strong enough to save us from the endless ingenuity of our hands.

Hummingbird
Tiny genius

The smallest bird of all is the bee humming-bird (*Mellisuga helenae*) and it weighs less than a penny. Despite being not much more than feathered wing muscles, the 320 species of hummingbird carry a huge amount of cerebral firepower. Relative to body size, their brains are twice as large as our own and this helps them do a number of things beyond the scope of larger animals.

Like us, they have a precise sense of time. The Rufous hummingbird (*Selasphorus rufus*) remembers not only where its food is located, but also when it last fed there. It will leave

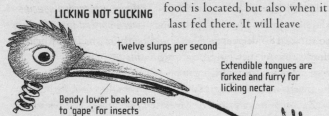

LICKING NOT SUCKING

Twelve slurps per second

Extendible tongues are forked and furry for licking nectar

Bendy lower beak opens to 'gape' for insects

flowers enough time to fill up with nectar before revisiting them. Hummingbirds are also one of only six groups of animals that learn how to communicate vocally, rather than just through instinct. Humans, whales and bats do this, but among other birds, it is only the parrots and songbirds that learn by imitation. Special structures in the frontal lobes of the brain control vocal learning, and this skill seems to have evolved independently in all three bird groups. For hummingbirds, it is driven by the need to maintain strict territorial control. Their nectar-licking lifestyle requires so much energy that keeping the neighbours away from the food supply is essential to survival. Singing is the most efficient way of doing this.

Their unique ability to feed from flowers while hovering also requires special brain adaptations. They can see much further into the ultraviolet spectrum than other birds (perhaps to help with flower recognition) and have a large section of brain dedicated to the visual adjustment that allows them to focus, despite the airflow created by having wings that beat up to 200 times a second. This also creates astonishing physical demands, so as well as being clever, hummingbirds have the largest heart relative to size, and the fastest metabolism, of any animal. In a single minute, their hearts can beat up to 1,200 times and they may take as many as 500 breaths.

Their flying technique is closer to a bumblebee's than to that of other birds, with ball-and-socket shoulder joints allowing their wings to rotate 180 degrees in all directions. As they hover the wing-tips move horizontally, tracing a figure-of-eight pattern rather than up and down, as with most birds. This means they can generate lift on both strokes, enabling them to fly forwards, backwards, and even upside down. To keep this up, they need to eat at least their own body-weight in nectar (for energy) and insects (for protein) every day. That means visiting an average of 1,500 flowers. Because this generates so much liquid waste, hummingbirds are continually dripping urine.

Their tiny feet are useless on the ground so they spend three-quarters of the day perching to save energy. At night, some species go into an energy-efficient torpor – a kind of mini-hibernation – where their metabolism plummets and their body temperature almost halves.

Hummingbird feathers come in two basic colours: reddish-brown and black. The amazing range of colours we see is caused by granules of melanin and tiny air bubbles in the feathers that refract light to create a metallic sheen. Light must shine on an iridescent feather at the correct angle, or we only see the dull 'pigment' colours.

> *The craze for hummingbird 'skins' for hats and bags peaked in the late nine-teenth century; one London dealer imported over 400,000 in a single year. Many unrecorded species were hunted to extinction until it was finally made illegal in 1918.*

Hyena
Girls on top

The female Spotted hyena (*Crocuta crocuta*) carries something between its legs that continues to baffle and fascinate biologists: a clitoris that matches the male's penis in shape, size and erectness. Its vagina is fused shut, so it uses this one organ to urinate, mate and give birth. How and why it has evolved may seem hard to fathom, not least because giving birth often results in painful tearing which kills one in ten mothers and often suffocates the first-born cub, whose umbilical cord is too short to negotiate the elongated birth canal. The usual assumption is that testosterone 'leaks' from male siblings in the womb, dousing the females, as sometimes happens to produce 'butch' female mice. But there is little evidence for this in spotted hyenas, and all females are similarly endowed.

> The ancient Egyptians trapped hyenas as pets and fattened them for the table. In the Ethiopian city of Harar, 'hyena-men' still feed on wild hyenas at dusk, holding the meat in their mouths.

The key is social organisation. Hyenas live in female-dominated societies, where every member in a clan has a precise hierarchical rank, with females being senior to males, and the female rank being inherited through the mother. This matriarchal social structure rivals those of the higher primates in complexity. In hunting terms, it delivers numerous benefits. A clan will chase their prey for miles, if necessary, until the target animal simply gives up. At that point the hyenas tear into its belly and legs, starting to eat it while it is still alive. This requires co-ordination and planning, but, above all, tremendous aggression. That's where the testosterone comes in handy. From birth, spotted hyenas are programmed to fight and a cub will often kill its twin (they are born in pairs) to establish dominance.

Spotted hyenas are Africa's dominant predator, responsible for a quarter of all game animals killed. Lions are their only rivals and the two species exist in a constant state of war. Both steal food from each other, but contrary to popular belief, lions scavenge more often from hyenas. In many areas, hyena kills are a lion's main source of food. Hyenas eat fast, and they eat a lot – a third of their own body-weight, or the size of large lamb, in just half an hour. They devour everything: the concentrated hydrochloric acid in their guts digests even the skin and bones, leaving their scat white with calcium.

For centuries, hyenas have been feared as corpse-eating grave robbers, sexual perverts and cowards. This human dislike of hyenas has ancient roots. The earliest hominid remains in northern Europe from 700,000 years ago are usually found close to hyena-gnawed bones and fossilised droppings. Whether as scavengers or as hunters, our species has evolved in close competition with hyenas.

Their eerily human-sounding 'laugh' is really a signal of submissiveness to clan superiors. Hyenas also whoop, to communicate over long distances. It's often the laugh or whoop which alerts other animals to come and poach their kill. At least one study has suggested that human music began with the collective hunting chants our ancestors used to 'outsing' the ancient enemy.

Hyenas aren't related to dogs: their closest relative is the cat-like civet. All four modern species, including the termite-eating aardwolf, are endangered through habitat loss and persecution by superstitious humans.

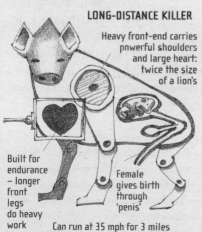

LONG-DISTANCE KILLER

Heavy front-end carries powerful shoulders and large heart: twice the size of a lion's

Built for endurance – longer front legs do heavy work

Female gives birth through 'penis'

Can run at 35 mph for 3 miles

Kangaroo
Bouncing desert cow

Imagine what it must have been like being confronted with a kangaroo for the first time. Here's Captain Cook in 1770: 'It was of a light mouse colour and the full size of a greyhound . . . I should have taken it for a wolf or a wild dog but for its walking or running which it jumped like a hare or deer.' So familiar have kangaroos become that we forget just how different they are from other mammals. A jumping dog with the eyes of a deer, the nose of a hare and the feet of a gerbil. How did it come about?

Marsupials or 'pouched animals' have ploughed their own furrow for 120 million years, but the large kangaroos (Macropods or 'big-feet') are a relatively recent development. The earliest fossils are 15 million years old, from the time Australia's forests began to recede. Until then, the kangaroos' ancestors had been non-hopping creatures of the woods — there was even a carnivorous sabre-toothed version.

The kangaroo's reproductive organs are worth a detour. The male has his testicles hanging above his penis and the female has three vaginas. It's perfectly logical. One is for birth, the other two are for sex: they carry the sperm to the two wombs.

Kangaroos adapted to become grass-grazing ruminants, the marsupial equivalents of bison and antelopes, and, like their placental counterparts, they grew larger to house a digestive system that could handle a tough, fibrous diet. Both their stomachs and their large intestines are fermenting vats full of bacteria and enzymes but, unlike cows, they produce not the greenhouse gas methane but another carbon-hydrogen compound: acetate, which they can recycle as energy. Kangaroo gut bacteria may yet help save the planet by producing wind-free cows.

Surviving in the hot, dry outback is all about conserving energy. Hopping is not only fast: it uses less energy than any other mode of transport. To avoid the daytime heat, kangaroos feed at night (hence their large eyes) and spend their days lying in the shade and licking their forearms to cool down. Even the remarkable reproductive system helps. Kangaroos, famously, have short pregnancies, with the tiny jellybaby-sized foetus crawling into its mother's pouch when only a month old. Less well known is the fact that a female kangaroo can store her embryos for many months in one of her two wombs. This not only means she can swiftly replace a joey that dies; she can also time her births to avoid droughts, saving both energy and water.

This rather undermines the view that marsupial reproduction is 'less advanced' than that of placental mammals. The tiny foetus may be underdeveloped but it has what it needs – functioning nostrils to smell the teat and two strong forelimbs to get it there in less than three minutes. (Incidentally, this is why marsupials never developed an aquatic species like whales or dolphins – no gripping arms: no babies.) Once safely in the pouch, the joey latches on, but is too weak to suck: the teat muscle exercises its own portion control, squirting just the right amount of rich milk into its mouth. The mother cleans the pouch, licking up the waste and thereby recycling a third of the milk she produces. When the fully grown joey is kicked out to make way for a new sibling, eight months later, it continues to suckle for several months. Ever mindful of waste, the mother kangaroo's mammary glands produce full-cream and fat-free milk simultaneously.

BIG FEET, SMALL CARBON FOOTPRINT

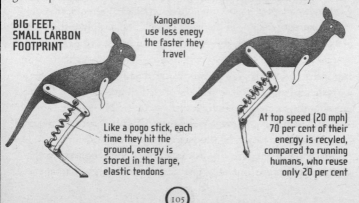

Kangaroos use less enegy the faster they travel

Like a pogo stick, each time they hit the ground, energy is stored in the large, elastic tendons

At top speed (20 mph) 70 per cent of their energy is recyled, compared to running humans, who reuse only 20 per cent

Koala
Cuddly bottom-feeder

Several mammals eat their own droppings, or their offspring's, but only koalas feed them to their young. The mother produces a soup, known as 'pap', which the four month-old joeys slurp up, ingesting important micro-organisms and preparing their delicate digestive tracts for the adult diet, which consists entirely of eucalyptus leaves.

Most herbivores don't go near eucalyptus. The leaves are 50 per cent water and contain nasty toxins. But the koala's guts have adapted to process them and they feed on only thirty of the 600 eucalyptus species that live in Australia; they can even tell the age of the leaves by their smell. To qualify as lunch they have to be between a year and eighteen months old, as young leaves have almost no nutritional value and older leaves contain poisonous prussic acid. On the plus side, koalas hardly ever have to drink – they get all the moisture they need from the leaves – but eucalyptus is so low in energy that they spend twenty hours a day asleep, like sloths. This might also explain why they have, pro-portionally, one of the smallest mammalian brains. Brains burn energy. The koala's occupies only half its cranial cavity, floating in fluid like a prune.

'Koala' means 'no water' in the Dharuk language. The Dharuk who lived around Sydney and Botany Bay are all long since extinct. 'Boomerang', 'dingo', 'wallaby' and 'coo-ee!' all come from the Dharuk.

Not even sex distracts them from sleep for long. It's very straightforward and takes place on a sturdy branch. The male mounts from behind, bites the female's neck and manages about forty thrusts of his bifurcated penis in twenty seconds. Once thrusting stops, ejaculation (into both vaginas) lasts for thirty seconds.

This perfunctory attitude might throw some light on the female koala's enthusiastic, if mysterious, adoption of lesbian behaviour when taken into captivity. Romps involving up to five females are commonplace, and outnumber heterosexual encounters by 3 to 1. They also last twice as long. Unfortunately, wild lesbian sex only helps to spread chlamydia, a sexually transmitted bacterial infection which afflicts three-quarters of all female koalas. Also known as 'wet bottom', it makes them smell bad and leaves them sterile.

Wild koalas are now officially listed as 'low risk to near-threatened'. Although aboriginal peoples did occasionally eat them, they didn't hunt them to near extinction as was once claimed: their population at the time Europeans arrived is estimated at ten million.

THE EUCALYPTUS GUT-BUSTER

Big nose for sniffing out poison

1 lb of leaves a day

Molars that shear instead of crush

10-foot Caecum, the largest of any mammal – four times longer than its body, surface area (12 square feet) full of fermenting leaves and bacteria

8 oz dry pellets or loose pap

What nearly did for them was the fur trade. Until it was banned in 1927, millions of skins were exported each year. Now, despite their iconic status, the koala population may be as low as 100,000, bush fires and road traffic having taken a heavy toll. The Australian Koala Foundation estimates that 80 per cent of their natural territory has been destroyed.

The koala's scientific name, *Phascolarctos cinereus*, means 'ash-grey pouch-bear' but koalas aren't bears; they are marsupials, close relatives of the wombat.

They have fingerprints that are almost indistinguishable from human ones. All primates have ridged finger-ends to help them climb, but marsupials split from the lineage of primates 125 million years ago, before koalas had evolved. The fact that two lineages independently developed the same trait to do the same job is a good example of 'convergent evolution'.

Komodo Dragon
Big and bad-mouthed

Ten feet long and weighing up to 20 stone, the komodo dragon (*Varanus komodoensis*) is already the largest living lizard. Now it holds he distinction of being the largest land animal capable of parthenogenesis (Greek for 'virgin birth').

In 2006, two of the three komodos held in UK zoos gave birth despite having had no access to a male. They managed this by a process called 'selfing'. In komodos, as in birds (but unlike mammals), it is the female who holds two different sex chromosomes: Z for male and W for female. Each of her ZW eggs has a second mini-egg attached to it, containing a full copy of her genetic information. In the absence of sperm, this gets re-absorbed and 'fertilizes' the main egg, producing a set of male (ZZ) non-identical twins.

This may have evolved as a survival strategy. Komodos are excellent swimmers and are only found on a few small islands in the middle of the Indonesian archipelago. A stranded female could populate a new island by mating with her own offspring.

The komodo was first discovered by Western scientists in 1910, despite the many local stories of a fierce dragon that lived in the island forests. In 1926, W. Douglas Burden, a wealthy adventurer, led an expedition to capture a live specimen. He failed, but his account of the trip inspired the Hollywood producer Merian C. Cooper to make the film *King Kong* in 1933.

Komodos are often called 'living dinosaurs', but unlike birds and crocodiles they aren't direct descendants. Komodos are monitor lizards, closely related to iguanas and snakes. They are fearsome carnivores, with flat serrated teeth (more like a shark's than a reptile's) and powerful curved claws. Their bite is fatal and their 'killer saliva' is legendary – it contains fifteen virulent strains of harmful bacteria – but recent research has confirmed that komodos are also venomous, with powerful toxins being secreted from glands in the mouth.

As the top predator on their islands, their isolation has allowed them to grow huge. They originally evolved to prey on a now extinct breed of pygmy elephant but will cheerfully take down buffalo, deer, goats, or young komodos. To avoid this, the young spend their early life in the treetops, and when joining a communal kill take the precaution of rolling in the prey's droppings to make themselves as unappetising as possible to their older colleagues.

Komodos eat once a month, wolfing down three-quarters of their body weight in a single sitting. Afterwards, they lie in the warm sun to stimulate digestion and prevent the food rotting in their stomachs. Sex is predictably violent. Males rear up on their hind legs and wrestle to establish dominance and, having succeeded, restrain the female just long enough to insert one of their two penises in her bottom.

They are highly intelligent. Captive komodos recognise their keepers and can perform simple tricks. But keep your shoes on, as Phil Bronstein found out. The newspaper editor and sometime husband to Sharon Stone had his foot badly mauled by a 'tame' komodo at the Los Angeles zoo in 2001.

KOMODOS SMELL WITH THEIR TONGUES

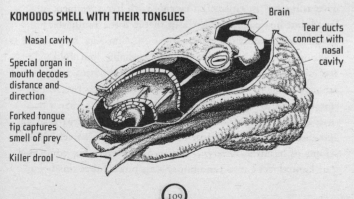

Brain

Tear ducts connect with nasal cavity

Nasal cavity

Special organ in mouth decodes distance and direction

Forked tongue tip captures smell of prey

Killer drool

Leech
A barometer that bites

There are 650 known species of leech. They are annelids: very close, but more sophisticated, relatives of the earthworm. Although they range in size from tiny to more than 18 inches in length, all leeches have thirty-four segments, each with its own 'brain'. The head segment contains a simple two-lobed structure, while the others have a clump of neurons called a *ganglion* (Greek for 'a swelling'). A single leech survives on a mere 15,000 neurons (honey bees' brains contain 950,000).

All leeches are carnivores, but very few species suck blood. The most famous is the European medicinal leech, *Hirudo medicinalis*. They have three muscular jaws, each of which has a row of tiny teeth. These saw into the skin, severing the capillaries beneath. The jaws sit at the centre of a powerful sucker which creates a vacuum around the wound, funnelling the blood into the leech's gut. Leeches feed for up to an hour, swelling to between five and ten times their original size and guzzling as much as a tablespoon of blood. When full, they drop off, leaving a Y-shaped puncture wound, rather like the Mercedes badge. They can live for up to six months on a single meal.

Leech bites do not hurt, but they can bleed for ten hours. This is because leech saliva contains both an anaesthetic and *hirudin*, an anticoagulant. Without it, the leech would end up resembling a chubby blood sausage.

Leech gatherers used to stand in lakes and pools, waiting for leeches to attach to their legs.

Leeches were probably first used in medicine in India around 1000 BC. The practice of bloodletting was used in the ancient Aztec, Babylonian, Egyptian and Greek cultures. Hippocrates taught that it helped restore an imbalance of the 'four humours' – blood, phlegm, black bile and yellow bile. By the nineteenth century, the use of leeches in medicine was so widespread that France imported more than forty-two million in 1833 alone. By the end of the century they were collected almost to extinction. Today, they have the same protected status as the white rhino.

The use of the leech in surgery is back with a vengeance. They are used in burns units and in plastic surgery for their blood-draining and anticoagulant properties. They can also reduce the painful inflammation of osteoarthritis and bruises. British hospitals buy 15,000 farmed leeches every year.

Don't try to remove an attached leech by burning it or pouring on salt. This will make it regurgitate into the wound, causing infection. Use a fingernail to slide under each of the suckers in turn. If you are unlucky enough to have a leech attached inside your mouth, gargle with vodka.

In 1799, Napoleon's troops in Sinai drank water contaminated by leeches. These attached themselves to the insides of the soldiers' noses, mouths and throats, killing hundreds through suffocation.

Leeches can predict thunderstorms. The change in atmospheric pressure means the water they swim in dissolves less oxygen, encouraging them to move to the surface. George Merryweather's Tempest Prognosticator, an elaborate leech barometer, was one of the wonders of the Great Exhibition in London in 1851.

Leech neurons have been used to construct a organic computer called the 'leech-ulator'. The device asks the neurons to perform simple sums. Unlike silicon processors, the neurons 'think' their answer by forming their own connections, one to another.

TEMPEST PROGNOSTICATOR

The machine consists of twelve bottles, each containing rain water and a leech

Bell rings when chain pulled down

Chain attached to lever

leech

Leech pushing upwards pulls down lever

As a storm approaches, leech ascends to the top of the bottle and rings a bell

Lion
Sub-Saharan couch potato

It's not easy being a male lion. Although they are the only cats to have adopted social organisation over solitary predation, it's not immediately obvious what benefits it brings. Most of their hunting isn't co-operative: it only becomes so if the pride is desperate and facing starvation. Even when it is, a single lion has to make the kill, and statistically that's usually a lioness, because they are faster and more agile. At mealtimes, all social cohesion dissolves; it's every lion for itself, and while the males hog the carcass, fights break out all round: flailing paws, shredded ears, mewling cubs and lionesses staking their claim by clamping their jaws on the carcass and refusing to budge.

Nor does the pride system seem particularly good at protecting the young. Only 10 per cent of cubs make it beyond the age of two; those that survive are lucky to get into double figures: a lion's life expectancy is much lower than that of the antelopes it chases. It's just not a healthy way to live, combining a high-fat diet with almost no exercise. The short sprints the lions make when hunting, while

Lions were widespread in Europe and Asia until relatively recently – the last lion was killed in the Caucasus in the tenth century, in Turkey in the late nineteenth century and in Iran in 1941. The last 300 wild Asiatic lions live in the Gir Forest in Gujarat, northern India.

being absolutely exhausting, are not the sort of sport which doctors recommend for anything, let alone someone suffering from high cholesterol. And then there's the stress.

If a male lion isn't avoiding the hoofs of zebras he's attempting to kill, or keeping other lions and hyenas off his dinner, he's either sleeping or servicing the insatiable demands of one of the pride's lionesses. When a female lion comes on heat, the male is looking at four days of pretty constant shagging – up

ROAR POWER

Lions can roar but not purr. Unlike in cats, their throat bones aren't solid – they're connected by an elastic ligament which allows their larynx to expand and vibrate

Lions roar to communicate with each other, not to intimidate prey

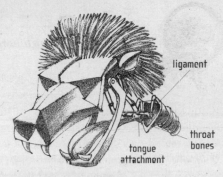

ligament

throat bones

tongue attachment

to fifty times a day. It's estimated for every cub that survives a year, its parents will have had 3,000 intimate encounters. It's not immediately obvious why: the female may need lots of spiny penis action to stimulate ovulation, as with domestic cats, or she could be just making sure her old man's up to the job.

Each pride consists of closely related females, serviced by a small coalition of unrelated males. These coalitions are regularly tested by outsiders, often younger males who are keen, in the heady flush of youth, to have a pride of their own. Just to be sure, a lioness will occasionally sneak off for some illicit action with one of these rogues. This leads to conflict, which among lions can be very nasty, even fatal. It certainly is for the cubs if the new team wins: the first thing they do is kill, and sometimes eat, the departing coalition's offspring. No wonder most coalitions last less than three years: it's too much like hard work.

Even the lion's mane – that universal symbol of virility – means something different to a lioness. Sporting a big, dark mane doesn't make you a breeding hero; in fact, as a fifty-a-day beast, you're probably history – manes are the leonine equivalent of nostril hair. But the absolute sign of a lion having given up trying to cut it as an apex predator or the King of the Jungle is when he turns man-eater. Slow, weak and always hanging around, we are easy prey: the lion's equivalent of a night in front of the TV with beer and a pizza.

No smoothen the lion.
CZECH ZOO SIGN

Lizard
Pleasantly reptilian

When the remains of the giant reptiles of the Mesozoic era were first discovered, Sir Richard Owen dubbed them 'dinosaurs' from the Greek *deinos sauros*, 'terrible lizard'. Encountering crocodilians in the New World, the Spanish called them *el lagarto de Indias*, 'the lizard of the Indies'. This became 'alligator' in English. But though there are more than 4,675 species of lizard, dinosaurs and alligators are not among them. Lizards are the reptile equivalent of rodents, found all over the world. They have a 'third eye' in the centre of their heads beneath the skin; they smell using their tongues and the cracks in their bottoms go sideways. Some are legless and distinguishable from snakes only by their movable eyelids, which snakes do not have.

The biggest group of lizards are skinks. They have tails with special fracture points. If a predator grabs them, their tails snap off and wriggle convulsively for several minutes, distracting the predator and giving the skink time to escape. The legless Glass lizards are even more dramatic: their tails shatter like glass if they're assaulted. Armadillo lizards (*Cordylus cataphractus*) roll into balls; blue-tongued skinks stick their tongues out; horned lizards squirt blood from their eyes. Australian frilled lizards

AUTOTOMATIC PILOT (Autotomy = 'self-cut')

Lizards are able to shed their tails because of a fracture plane across (or between) their tail vertebrae. The muscles contract above it to snap off the tail and then act as sphincters to seal the tail artery

The tail grows back around a tube of cartilage, not a bone

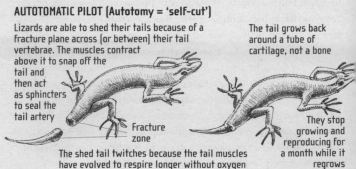

Fracture zone

The shed tail twitches because the tail muscles have evolved to respire longer without oxygen

They stop growing and reproducing for a month while it regrows

(*Chlamydosaurus kingii*) have a pleat of skin around their necks. When they are threatened, this opens out like a golf umbrella, making them seem much larger than they are. The flying dragons (*Draco volans*) of South-East Asia leap from trees, gliding to safety on brightly coloured parachutes. And lizards also escape by running – though none quite so stylishly as the basilisk, or Jesus Christ lizard (*Basiliscus basiliscus*), which has large

> Nile monitor lizards cunningly lay their eggs in termite mounds. The termites repair the damage around the eggs and the heat of the mound incubates them.

webbed hind feet, enabling it to stand up and walk on water. The fastest lizards are six-lined racerunners (*Cnemidophorus sexlineatus*): at 18 mph they are the fastest reptiles on earth. Only one lizard lives in the sea: the Galápagos marine iguana (*Amblyrhynchus cristatus*), which dives 30 feet under water to nibble algae on the rocks. Some lizards are venomous but, luckily for humans, they secrete poison by chewing and need a good old gnaw to cause anything more than a mild swelling. The heaviest lizard is the 20-stone Komodo dragon; the lightest is a dwarf gecko so tiny it would fit on your fingertip.

Geckos are popular house guests in hot countries because they eat insects at night. Brook's half-toed gecko of West Africa (*Hemidactylus brookii*) even has a transparent belly to advertise to its hosts how many flies it has caught. Geckos can walk vertically up glass and scientists have recently discovered how. Their feet are covered in half a million tiny hairs, each of which splits into hundreds more with diameters less than the wavelength of light. This creates a powerful bond between the electrons in the two surfaces. Half a square inch of adhesive tape based on this principle has already been manufactured. If enough can be made to cover a human hand, you could hang by it from the ceiling. In China, lizard soup is used as medicine for asthma, colds, lungs and the heart. In Antigua, lizard soup is also said to be good for asthma. Provided the patient isn't told what's in it. Apparently. that just makes it worse.

Lobster
The swimming locust

The name lobster comes from the Old English *loppestre*, the product of a collision between the Latin for locust (*locusta*) and *loppe*, Old English for spider. As arthropods, they are closely related to both. The best-known lobsters are the European and the American, but there are about fifty species including the Hunchback locust lobster, the Velvet fan lobster and the Musical furry lobster. Lobsters from 140 million years ago were so like today's that if you ate one for dinner you wouldn't notice the difference.

Lobsters are surprisingly fast swimmers: with a flex of their tail they can shoot along at 15 feet a second. Some have been tracked covering distances of over a hundred miles a year, in search of food and sex. Lobster sex involves a lot of undressing and urination. Like mice, they use their urine to communicate. Their two bladders are handily located in their heads, so urine can be mixed with water and squirted from their gills into the face of a potential mate. Male and female lobsters usually attack each other on sight, but, luckily, male lobsters find the urine of a moulting female arousing. Males wait in their rock shelters, urinating out of the doorway. Females approach when ready to moult, and urinate back at them. They have sex in the missionary position: the male props open the female's sperm pouch with his swimming legs and, after some leg-fanning foreplay, ejaculates gelatinous sperm capsules into her pouch. He protects her until her shell hardens — about two weeks later — and then hostilities resume.

> Lobsters are peaceful, serious creatures, who know the secrets of the sea, and don't bark.
> GERARD DE NERVAL

To grow, a lobster must shed its shell. Because the food-grinding teeth inside its stomach are part of the exoskeleton, it has to pull out the lining of its throat, stomach and anus to free itself. Not all lobsters survive this process. It also makes it hard to tell their age. Many of the ones we eat are over twenty years old, but a big specimen can weigh as much as a labrador and may have lurked on the ocean floor for over a century.

The pincher claw tears

The larger, stronger crushing claw holds tight

Fighting lobsters lock crushing claws until one of them submits. Sometimes, they attack each other's antennae, legs, claws or eyes. A large crusher claw can exert as much as 1,000 lb per square inch on something small (like a human finger). To escape, they can jettison a limb using a special muscle at its base but because lobsters' blood flows through their body cavities, not veins, they will bleed to death unless leaks are sealed quickly. Legs, antennae and claws can regenerate, but not eyes.

As long as their gills are damp, lobsters can breathe. They will survive for up to a week out of water. French Romantic poet Gérard de Nerval used to take Thibault, his pet lobster, for walks in Paris using a blue ribbon as a lead.

Cooked lobsters are red because boiling transforms protein molecules in the shell into shapes that absorb everything except red light, which is reflected. There is no clear evidence about whether lobsters feel pain. Boiling water is probably the quickest method but there is no absolutely humane way of killing them.

'Bloody filthy lobster again . . .'

Early New England settlers considered lobsters barely edible. When storms blew them on to the beach, farmers used them for animal feed or fertiliser and served them only as food for prisoners

Louse
Intimate informant

Lice are very small wingless insects, related to the bugs, aphids and cicadas. They live as parasites in the fur or feathers of mammals and birds, feeding on blood, dead skin or feather parts. Almost all animal species support one or two varieties, living on different parts of their body. Notable exceptions are bats, platypuses and echidnas, which are louse-free.

Humans carry three lice species: on our heads, our clothes and our pubes. By studying their DNA alongside those of other primates, we've learnt rather a lot about ourselves. The pubic louse (*Pthirus pubis*), for example, is very closely related to the gorilla louse (*Pthirus gorillae*). The DNA shows the two species split over three million years ago, so our hominid ancestors either occasionally slept with gorillas, or used abandoned gorilla nests as hammocks. Similar analysis of head lice (*Pediculus humanus capitis*) tells us that we split from chimpanzees five and a half million years ago, and that we caught a second species from the heads of our now extinct cousins, *Homo erectus*, three million years later. Body lice (*P. humanus humanus*) live only on clothing and evolved from head lice about 70,000 years ago, thus telling us when we first started getting dressed.

THE LOUSE CANNON

To hatch, lice nymphs suck air into the egg

Pressure builds until the egg's cap blows ...

PAF!

... and the young louse is fired out

A week later they can call themselves adults

Adult lice look like tiny crabs, hence their nickname. They have powerful pincers on their front legs, which they use to anchor themselves close to their host's skin, by grabbing hair or feather barbs. The shape of some bird lice has evolved to fit exactly in between the barbs so they can't be removed by preening (which is why birds have dust baths).

Lice can't jump, so you need contact to catch them. Some bird lice hitch a ride with a passing fly if their host dies or becomes too crowded. As a means of distribution, this is risky, as they can't live on the fly. Most lice can only survive for a day or two if separated from their host. One of the least remarked-upon mass extinctions of recent times was that of the passenger pigeon louse, *Lipercus extinctus*. When the pigeons died out, so did the louse. Similarly, the programme to protect and breed Californian condors in captivity inadvertently destroyed the condor-chewing louse (*Colpocephalum californici*), when the remaining birds were all fumigated.

Sometimes lice do switch species. The dog louse (*Heterodoxus spiniger*) infests dogs everywhere except Europe, but it evolved in Australia to feed on wallabies and only moved to dingos when they arrived with Indonesian fishermen 4,000 years ago.

Some lice are actively harmful: the faeces of the human body louse carry typhus and trench fever viruses. Analysis of the lice found on the buried remains of French soldiers who died in Napoleon's retreat from Moscow confirms that lice killed more of them than the Russians did.

The 'nits' that children catch from each other are the eggs of the head louse, which the louse sticks to the base of the hair using a special cement. It's so strong that some females end up sticking themselves to a strand of hair and starving to death. They lay six eggs a day. The optimum population is about a hundred lice per head, which takes about a month to build up.

There is only one species of louse that is officially classified as 'endangered', the pygmy hog sucking louse (Haematopinus oliveri), attached to the dwindling pygmy hog population of the Indian savannah.

Mite

Invisible lodger

Mites are tiny, eight-legged members of the spider clan but most are too small for us to see. After insects, they are the most diverse group of animals on the planet. We don't know how many species of mite there are; over 48,000 have been identified so far, but this is probably only a tenth of the total number. They can live almost anywhere, on land or sea, from the icy, sunless ocean depths to hot springs where the temperature would boil most other organisms. Only bacteria are more adaptable; mites can raise a family in the windpipe of the honey bee, or hitch lifts between flowers on the beak of a hummingbird. A single square foot of forest contains a million mites from over 200 different species.

Not that you have to go as far as the woods. As you read this, the follicle mite, *Demodex folliculorum*, is using its needle-shaped jaws to feast on the oil from the sebaceous glands at the base of your eyelashes. Demodex mites look like chubby toothbrushes, with a long abdomen and four pairs of clawed legs. They burrow into the follicle headfirst and have a digestive system so efficient they don't produce any waste. When they die, they just dissolve *in situ*, with no harmful side effects.

IN-YOUR-FACE INCEST

Human eyelash

The female follicle mite produces her first litter without mating

She mates with her new sons a week later to produce twenty-five more eggs

The new generation, in turn, crawl off at night to find their own follicles

Up to ten mites burrow into skin around eyelash

Their 'bottoms' stick out as mites lodge into eyelash base

Our homes are vast continents teeming with independent mite

kingdoms: flour mites, cheese mites, furniture mites, prune mites, mould mites, each feeding and reproducing in its own microhabitat. Probably the most infamous is the dust mite (*Dermatophagoides pteronyssinus* – or 'skin-eating feather-stabber') They don't feed on humans but on the flakes of skin that fall from our bodies. Considering each of us produces a small flour bag's worth of skin flakes a year, there's plenty for them to chew on. The musty smell that hits us when we empty our

> *Demodex means 'lard worm'. The notorious nineteenth-century biologist Sir Richard Owen, better-known for inventing the term 'dinosaur', named it.*

vacuum cleaner is caused by the digestive enzymes of dust mites: half a teaspoon of dust contains as many as a thousand mites and 250,000 pellets of their droppings. Although these droppings can aggravate asthma, caution is needed: dust mites do an important job ridding our environment of scurf and dander. Also, they are *impossible* to remove in the long term. Obsessive vacuuming just redistributes them and their eggs around the house and, worse still, sucks up their main predator, the larger *Cheyletus* mite that helps keep their population stable. Carpet cleaning is an even happier prospect: it creates just the warm, moist conditions in which they thrive (which is why they like our mattresses so much).

That's not to undermine the threat posed by mites and their subfamily, the ticks. They carry viruses on their bodies and in their saliva which cause scabies, Lyme disease, dermatitis and typhus in humans and mange in animals; a single species, *Varroa destructor*, came close to wiping out the world's honey bee population. By far the largest number of mite species feed on plants and their effect on crops can be devastating, causing billions of pounds worth of damage each year. But the mites' diversity may their Achilles' heel. Even mites themselves have mites. In 2001, the green mite that had decimated the African cassava crop was arrested by the import of a predatory mite from Brazil, the plant's original home.

Mole
The all-seeing nose

Moles aren't blind, but their pinhead eyes can only tell light from dark. What really sets them apart is their noses, which they use for 'feeling' rather than smelling.

The nose of the Star-nosed mole (*Condylura cristata*) is unique. It looks like a pink sea anemone, but is really a twenty-two fingered, non-grasping hand that the mole uses to form a complete picture of its underground world. With a much higher density of nerve-endings than the average clitoris, it uses a similar brain capacity to that used for sight in other mammals, making it more of an eye than a hand.

'Mole' comes from 'mouldwarp', Old English for 'earth-thrower'. The dialect name was 'woont', molecatchers were 'woonters' and molehills were 'woonty-tumps'.

The Star-nosed mole holds two other records. It has the fastest reactions of any mammal: locating, identifying and eating an insect larva in an average of 227 milliseconds, which is less time than it takes to read the word 'mole' and three times faster than most of can us brake at a red light. It is also the only mammal to 'smell' under water, sprouting large air bubbles from its nostrils rather like a child blowing bubblegum.

If a mole goes without a meal for eight hours, it dies. The diet of the European mole (*Talpa europaea*) consists chiefly of earthworms: their tunnels are traps for worms to fall into. They need to eat about a hundred each day. By biting their heads to immobilise them, a mole can keep up to 500 worms alive in underground 'larders'. Moles drink a lot, too, and at least one of their tunnels will come out by a ditch or pond. Contrary to myth, they do not eat plant roots or other vegetable matter.

If short of worms, a mole might dig 150 feet of new tunnels in a day, the equivalent of a human moving four tons (about a thousand shovel loads) every twenty minutes.

Moles are not nocturnal — it's just that we rarely see them. In fact, they work in shifts alternating four hours of frantic digging and eating with four hours of sleep. They are highly territorial and solitary, each animal's territory covering anything up to four football pitches. This solitary life is only relieved for the few hours each spring when they come together to mate, which sometimes happens above ground.

For the rest of the year, moles use their forty-four teeth to make sure other individuals keep their distance. This includes the females, who are equipped with another mammalian first: a pair of ovaries-cum-testicles that release eggs in the spring and testosterone in the autumn, when they need to defend their ground. There are differences. Males are slightly larger and their tunnelling behaviour is different. Females build an irregular network, whereas males, of course, tunnel in long, straight lines.

Molehills consist of exceptionally fine soil, prized by gardeners as seed compost. In the second half of the nineteenth century, moleskin provided molecatchers with a very good income. It took a hundred skins to make a waistcoat, and by the turn of the century several million British moleskins were being exported to the USA annually.

The British mole population is now estimated at over thirty-five million. In 2002 the post of Mole-catcher Royal was revived with the appointment of Victor Williamson at Sandringham.

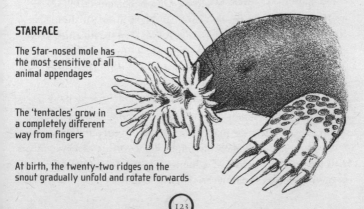

STARFACE

The Star-nosed mole has the most sensitive of all animal appendages

The 'tentacles' grow in a completely different way from fingers

At birth, the twenty-two ridges on the snout gradually unfold and rotate forwards

Monkey
Social tinker

Anyone who's taken children to a zoo will
know the tractor-beam-like attraction that
monkeys exert. A monkey enclosure is like a 12A movie – scenes
of mild peril with some sexual content. Children like monkeys
because they feel a direct connection with them, and they are
right: only the apes are closer relatives. It's interesting that
within a few decades of the word 'monkey' first being used
(1530, although its origin is obscure), we had already begun to
use it as an affectionate nickname for children.

Wherever they are found in the
world, monkeys live in big groups.
Their relatively large brains, and the
intelligence they confer, have enabled
them to cope with the complex interactions required to keep a social order
going. The more we learn about
monkey societies, the more they seem
like us. It's obviously going to delight
seven-year-old boys to discover that
among Angolan black-and-white

> *The White uakari is one
> of the oddest-looking
> of all monkeys. It lives
> in the Brazilian rain
> forest where its bald,
> bright-red face and
> rather human ears have
> earned it the nickname
> 'the Englishman'.*

colobus monkeys (*Colobus angolensis*), a burp is counted a friendly
greeting (like many monkeys they're leaf-eaters, so wind is a
constant in their lives). Also, the widespread use of grooming to
suck up to the dominant male has a definite schoolboy logic to
it, although most schoolboys stop short of removing dead skin
and lice from the playground bully.

More grown up human behaviour also finds its monkey
equivalent. Monkeys plan ahead: Grey-cheeked mangabeys
(*Lophocebus albigena*) make decisions based on the weather,
remembering the location of particularly good fig trees and
waiting for the sun to shine before setting out on fruit-picking
expeditions. Vervet monkeys (*Chlorocebus aethiops*) display a very

human attitude to booze. On the Caribbean island of St Kitts they have learnt to hang out near bars, and finish the cocktails people leave behind. The majority are social drinkers who imbibe in moderation with other monkeys. They prefer their alcohol to be diluted with fruit juice and never drink before lunch. Others refuse to drink at all, but 5 per cent are serious binge drinkers who consume as much hard liquor as they can, make a lot of noise, and start fights, before finally passing out.

Drunkenness is not the only vice we share. An experiment with rhesus macaques (*Macaca mulatta*) revealed that they would 'pay' to look at pictures of the faces and bottoms of high-ranking females by forfeiting their usual reward of a glass of cherry juice. With low-ranking females, however, the researchers had to bribe them with an even larger glass of juice before they'd pay any attention. Some species have even taken the law into their own hands. Pig-tailed macaques (*Macaca nemestrina*) 'elect' senior monkeys to break up fights and keep order. Their authority rarely requires the back-up of force, but as soon as the police monkeys are removed, cliques rapidly form and social cohesion breaks down.

For all the similarities there is a gulf between humans and monkeys that only our imaginations can fill. Macaques, smart as they are, know if we're imitating them but can't make the leap and imitate us back. A deep bond remains, nonetheless, and may even be hard-wired. A Canadian research team recently found that, up to the age of three months, newborn humans respond as positively to the calls of rhesus monkeys as they do to human speech.

FROM NOSE TO TAIL

 Nostrils spread out and wide

Grasping tail

Fingertip grip

 Non-grasping (or absent) tail

Calloused bottom pads

Nostrils close together and narrow

New World monkey (capuchin)　　**Old World monkey (mandrill)**

Moose
Lippy northern stripper

Moose (*Alces alces*) are, by a wide margin, the largest living members of the deer family. A bull moose weighs three times as much as a red deer stag. The weight of his antlers alone would exceed the personal baggage allowance on international flights (50 lb), and are wide enough for a child to sling a hammock between them. Moose have grown big to cope with the cold: they are only found in the high latitudes of the northern hemisphere. Big is better for keeping warm (a lower surface-area-to-volume ratio helps prevent heat loss), which is why so many ice-age mammals grew so large.

Moose have a double layer of insulating fur, and long legs for wading through snow; even their newborn calves seem happy in temperatures of −30° C. More troubling is warm weather: they can't sweat, and fermenting vegetation turns their stomach into a furnace. In winter, temperatures much above −5° C will set them panting or lying flat in the snow to cool down. During the summer they spend a lot of time wading in water for the same reason.

Moose are notoriously difficult to keep in captivity. Unlike most other deer, who can browse happily on twigs or graze grass, they are specialised feeders. An adult moose needs to eat the equivalent of a large straw bale of vegetation every day, chewing the cud like a cow to extract the maximum nutritional value. They eat leaves, bark and twigs during the autumn and winter for energy, and marsh plants, when they are in season during spring and early summer, for sodium. Commercial feed can't match this balance, so captive moose tend to die quite quickly. The need for salt explains why you often see them licking roads during the summer. It's also why moose

> *Moose antler is the fastest-growing animal tissue, sprouting an inch a day. Antlers are sensitive enough for the moose to feel a fly land on them.*

spend so much time in the water; aquatic plants like water lilies and horsetails are sodium-rich and moose will completely submerge themselves to graze on the bottom of ponds. Reports of them 'diving' are usually exaggerations: they are the wrong shape and size for serious underwater swimming.

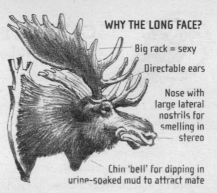

WHY THE LONG FACE?

Big rack = sexy

Directable ears

Nose with large lateral nostrils for smelling in stereo

Chin 'bell' for dipping in urine-soaked mud to attract mate

What they can do well is to strip trees with their large drooping upper lip (they have no upper front teeth) — the name 'moose' comes from the old Algonquian word *mooswa*, meaning 'the animal that strips bark off trees'. Their eyes can move independently, enabling them to see behind while still looking forward and the long nose, full of soft cartilage and muscle, is a hypersensitive food-finder-cum-sex aid. This nasal succulence wasn't lost on local Native American tribes. According to the eighteenth-century naturalist, Thomas Pennant, the moose's nose was the 'perfect marrow, and esteemed the greatest delicacy in all Canada'.

In Europe moose are called elks, from the Latin *alces*, and were first described by Julius Caesar in 50 BC. The elk became extinct in Britain in the Bronze Age but the name lived on and was used to describe any large deer. When English settlers reached America, the commonest deer, *Cervus canadensis*, reminded them of its British relative, the red deer (*Cervus elaphus*). As a result, it acquired the name 'elk' and the other huge and unfamiliar beast continued with its local name, 'moose'.

The size and shape of a moose makes them bad news in a collision, so Scandinavian car manufacturers test new models using an artificial moose. Swedish adverts disparage Japanese cars with the reminder: 'There are no moose in Japan'

Mouse
The furry weed

The histories of humans and house mice (*Mus musculus*) are inseparable. The original *Mus* had lived happily outdoors in northern India for millions of years but as soon as our hunter-gatherer ancestors started to farm in Mesopotamia 10,000 years ago, the mouse lifestyle was also transformed. Permanent houses and grain stores inadvertently provided reliable food and shelter and the small, swift, resourceful mouse needed no further encouragement. The very name 'mouse' (from Latin *mus* and Greek *mys*) ultimately derives from the Sanskrit root *mush*, which means mouse and also to steal. Hence wherever we went thereafter – on foot, in carts, or by ship – the little thief kept us company.

As a result, house mice can be found wherever there are settled populations of people (as well as many places where there are none). They live on all the continents; at altitudes as high as 15,600 feet; as far north as the Bering Sea; and as far south as the sub-Antarctic islands. They live in coal-mines, meat freezers, underground railway tunnels. This is partly because they can live on almost anything – seeds, roots, insects, larvae, food scraps – and if they need to drink at all, licking dew or condensation is enough. But the real source of their success is that they can rapidly adapt their behaviour to suit the environment they find themselves in. Most animals change slowly. Wherever we take them, mice not only survive: they find a way to thrive.

Their prodigious fertility helps. Mice are sexually mature at four weeks; a single pair of mice can produce 500 offspring in a year. It's a competitive business and female mice are extremely promiscuous. The bigger the penis, the longer and more frequent the copulation; and the higher the volume of ejaculate, the more likely conception is to occur. A quarter of all litters are the product of more than one father, a strategy that not only ensures genetic diversity but also helps to prevent any new male

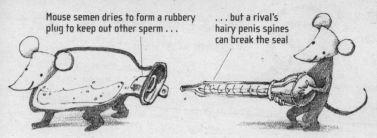

Mouse semen dries to form a rubbery plug to keep out other sperm . . .

. . . but a rival's hairy penis spines can break the seal

partner eating a female's offspring, just in case they are his. In extreme cases, she will even reabsorb the foetuses to prevent them being eaten.

Mouse sex is not without its romantic side. Male mice sing complex songs in ultrasound, both to attract mates and during the act itself. Slowed down, they sound disconcertingly like Clangers. Most murine communication is via urine, which they dab around continually. Age, sex, health and sexual status are all encoded in a mouse's urine 'signature'. Male scent is used territorially; female scent is to do with breeding, a kind of mousy 'girl talk'. It's one of the reasons mice dislike peppermint – it scrambles their communication network.

What do we get out of the relationship? House mice now comprise 98 per cent of all animals used in genetics research. Amazingly, most of these derive from just two breeding strains (C57BL/6 and L/10) sold to a laboratory in 1921 by Massachusetts schoolteacher and 'fancy mouse' breeder, Abbie Lathrop. Also, mice are what most carnivorous predators eat most of the time. This is a very good thing: if there weren't any mice, they would be forced to eat our livestock. Indeed, without the little thief, it is unlikely that the ancient Egyptians would have bothered domesticating cats in the first place.

Sanskrit has forty words for 'mouse'. Mushka is 'little mouse' but also means 'testicle'. From this, we get 'musk' (from the scrotum-like gland of the musk deer) and 'muscle' (from its mouse/testicle-like movement under the skin).

Naked Mole Rat
A termite with teeth

A strong contender for the planet's ugliest animal, the Naked mole rat looks like a flaccid penis with teeth. It is also one of the least well named, being neither naked, a mole, nor a rat. Cousin to the porcupine and the guinea pig, it is a 3-inch long rodent, which uses its huge incisors to carve out tunnels in the hard desert soil. Although it looks completely bald, it does have whiskers on its face and tail which act as navigational sensors, and hairy toes which sweep soil behind it like a broom.

They are the only mammals to live in organised colonies, like termites and bees. Only one female breeds, serviced by a harem of three males and supported by as many as 300 'workers' and 'soldiers', who divide the tunnelling, childcare, food collection and defence functions between them. This behaviour is called eusocial (*eu-* meaning 'good') and has evolved in response to the harsh conditions of their home territory in eastern Africa, where a lack of rain and food mean they need to cooperate to survive. A large colony gives them better odds of coming across the sparse underground vegetable tubers which cater for all their food and drink needs. By carefully boring into them, they can keep the tubers growing, providing a sustainable food source for years.

Naked mole rats feel no pain. They lack a neurotransmitter chemical called 'Substance P', which may be an adaptation helping them cope with the near poisonous levels of carbon dioxide in their stuffy burrows.

Naked mole rats (*Heterocephalus glaber*, the 'odd-headed smooth one') spend almost all their life underground. Their eyes have become so useless that they usually keep them closed. They can also close their lips behind their teeth, to keep their mouths free of soil while digging.

NAKED CHAIN GANG

Naked mole rats form digging gangs with specialised roles in order to shift the loose dirt out of their tunnels

Volcano

Volcanoer

Sweeper

Sweeper

Sweeper

Digger

Except for the queen and her harem, digging is what mole rats do. A quarter of their muscle is in the jaw, and a third of their brain is used to process information from their mouths. Colonies contain miles of tunnels; an individual worker can dig half a mile a month when the soil is softened by rain. That's equivalent to a human digging the 12 miles from central London to Heathrow Airport. Mole rats are practically cold-blooded: when they're not digging or eating, they sleep heaped together in communal chambers to keep warm.

As with other mammals, the newborns are suckled by the mother. The queen gives birth to between twenty and thirty 'pups' at a time, but only has twelve nipples – a unique mismatch for a mammal. Pups get their food by waiting patiently and taking turns.

Queen mole rats are fat bullies, nose-shoving the underlings when their work isn't up to snuff. A combination of work stress and intimidation seems to be enough to suppress the sex hormones in both male and female workers, although the queen supplements this with a special chemical in her urine, the equivalent of bromide in a soldier's tea. A 'sterile' worker that is removed from a colony becomes sexually active within a week.

A queen and her harem can live for twenty-five years, producing over a thousand offspring. When she dies, vicious fights break out between the largest remaining females to decide the next 'queen'. Mole rat colonies are like large, in-bred, dysfunctional families. The lack of interbreeding with other colonies means that the workers are propagating some of their own genes by helping to raise a conveyor belt of siblings.

Octopus
Well-armed

To look at, octopuses are about as different from humans as it's possible to imagine: no body to speak of, just a head sprouting eight arms (it's very biologically incorrect to call them legs or tentacles). So it's pleasing to discover that they have larger brains, relative to body weight, than any animals except birds and mammals, and that they get bored easily. If they are kept in environments enriched with natural features, they grow faster, learn faster and remember more of what they learn than if they are kept in bare tanks. They remember places where they might find food, and where they have already hunted. And although octopuses are mostly solitary, there is evidence that they can communicate and, if kept together, they establish hierarchies and avoid confrontations. For all these reasons, in the UK octopuses enjoy the same legal status in labs as vertebrates.

> Octopuses are good mimics. Some imitate other dangerous animals like sea snakes and lionfish. Others pretend to be drifting clumps of algae or water-logged coconuts.

What they are not so good at is recognising the sex of other octopuses (or octopodes, but never octopi: the word is derived from Greek, not Latin). Put two octopuses in a tank and they will start to copulate regardless of sex. Thirty seconds into a male-on-male encounter there's usually an unembarrassed disentangling, although some of these gay clinches can last for days. In one case, the two males weren't even from the same species. Despite Japanese artists' persistent obsession with giant octopuses pleasuring women in eight erogenous zones simultaneously, octopus sex is a polite affair, carried out at arm's length. One of the male's eight arms is for mating and it differs from the others by having a groove on its underside and a grasping tip called a ligula which in some species inflates with

THE OCTOPUS ELBOW

Despite having a completely flexible arm, an octopus forms three 'joints' to retrieve a piece of food, just like a vertebrate. This is the simplest, most efficient movement

Two-thirds of octopus neurons are in the arms' nerve cords. The nerve cord 'chooses' where the joints will go; the brain co-ordinates the movement

Joint 1 ('Wrist')

Joint 2 ('Elbow')

Joint 3 ('Shoulder')

blood, rather like a mammal's penis. The arm carefully places a packet of sperm in a corresponding slot in the female's mantle (the body/head). The ligula then breaks off and remains embedded in the female. The male dies within a few months of mating. Although octopuses can regenerate lost limbs, they can't grow a new sex arm.

The male blanket octopus takes sexual discretion to a new level. He is 40,000 times smaller than the female and his technique involves tearing off his mating arm, placing it somewhere on her body and then swimming off to die. Given that this is roughly equivalent to a herring nudging a blue whale, it's unlikely that she's even aware of him. Meanwhile his disengaged arm crawls into her gill slit, where it can live for as long as a month, until her eggs are mature. She then retrieves it, tears it open like a packet of café sugar and sprinkles the sperm over her eggs.

Octopuses are as dextrous as they are smart. They can open jam-jars, use stones as tools to open shells and wield snapped-off jellyfish tentacles as weapons. Some 'walk' on two arms, as if they were bipeds. They use their body muscles to squirt themselves forwards, reaching speeds of 25 mph. They can even 'fly' using this method – squirting themselves right out of the water to escape predators. As octopuses have no skeleton – the only hard part of an octopus is its parrot-like beak – they can squeeze through spaces as small as their eyeballs.

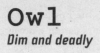

Owl
Dim and deadly

The large, slow-blinking eyes lend the owl's face an expressive quality most birds lack and this has doubtless contributed to its reputation for wisdom. In fact, an owl is not overburdened with brain. Its eyeballs are almost as large as a human's, even though its skull (without feathers) is barely the size of a golfball. This doesn't leave a lot of room for problem-solving. Owls look as they do because they are supremely well adapted for the job of catching small prey at night. Their huge pupils capture a lot of light and the eyeball is shaped like a café salt-shaker rather than a sphere to allow space for the largest possible retina. The retina itself has many more light-sensitive rods than detail-focusing cones, enabling owls to see

AVIAN IMAX

Supersized eyeballs provide multi-megapixel imaging with very little light. Offset ears complete the picture

'Uh-oh . . .'

when the light level falls to almost nothing. A long-eared owl's (*Asio otus*) eyes are so sensitive that it can locate a stationary mouse in light levels equivalent to a football stadium illuminated by a single candle. The downside of such big forward-facing eyes is that owls can't move them. If they want to change their range of view, they have to swivel their head. If they want to judge an object's position accurately, they bob their heads round, reading it from slightly different angles.

But eyes are only half the story. An owl's ears are, in contrast, very sensitive. The flat feather-dishes on its face help to capture sound waves like a pair of satellite bowls, channelling them to its ears, which are huge vertical slits running down both sides of the skull. Sometimes these are cock-eyed (or, rather, cock-eared) on the head, with one higher than the other, or else the owl can manipulate its ear-flaps to create different-sized openings. This allows it to calculate the precise location of its prey by estimating the tiny span of time it takes for the rustling sound of a mouse to get to each of its ears. It is accurate enough for some species to hunt in total darkness.

Owls' necks have fourteen vertebrae (twice as many as mammals) to allow the head to turn through 270°

As well as unusual sight and hearing, owls have evolved a unique system for silent flight. Their bodies and legs are covered with a great number of downy feathers, and even their flight feathers have unzipped, fringed ends to soften the flow of air over them. This makes them look a lot larger than they really are. The long-eared owl has a 3-foot wingspan but weighs less than an orange. To hide, it sucks in its feathers and manages a reasonable impression of a branch.

For a long time owls were grouped with falcons, but they now have their own order, *Strigiformes*, from *strix*, the Greek for 'owl' and the root of the word 'strident'. The name mimics the owl's sound, as does 'owl' itself – which comes from the Latin *ululatio*, 'a cry of lamentation'. The owl's cry and nocturnal habits associate it with omens of death and ill-fortune in almost every culture.

In India it is common to call a foolish person 'an owl' – owls are considered bad omens, messengers of ill luck, or servants of the dead.

135

Pangolin
Sacred pine cone

The relatively recent advances in molecular analysis which allow us to trace the family tree encoded in an animal's genes have thrown up numerous surprises, and nowhere more so than with the pangolin or 'scaly anteater', a strangely beguiling mammal that looks like a pine cone with legs. For a long time it was classified with the anteaters and armadillos, because it looks and acts like them. Yet its genes tell a different story: it is actually a carnivore, brother under its scales to cats, dogs and bears.

There are seven pangolin species, four in Africa, three in Asia, in their own order, the *Pholidota*, or 'horny-skinned ones'. All but two have prehensile (grasping) tails that enable them to climb trees. They are mostly nocturnal, emerging from their burrows at night to feed on ants and termites. Like the aardvark – to which they are not related – they operate mainly by smell, tearing open the nests with powerful claws and 'drinking' the residents in large gulps. The Giant pangolin (*Manis gigantea*) of Africa can extend its tongue 16 inches. When not in use it is rolled up in a sheath deep in the chest cavity, its powerful muscles anchored at the pelvis. The tongue is covered with incredibly sticky mucus, supplied by a large gland in the chest. They have no teeth but instead grind their food in their stomachs, swallowing small stones and sand, just as birds fill their gizzards.

In China pangolin are known as 'hill carp' and their flesh is a delicacy fetching more than £20 a pound. The animals are killed to order in restaurants, the warm blood drunk as a tonic.

Pangolins have a curious walk, slowly ambling on all fours by resting their front knuckles on the ground and curving the claws underneath. When they want to speed up they walk on their hind legs, rolling forwards, balanced by their tail. A hungry pangolin can wipe out an insect colony in thirty minutes. They are highly intelligent predators; if a termite nest proves too big to finish off in one go, they will seal it up and return the following day.

'Pangolin' comes from the Malay *peng goling*, meaning 'something that rolls up'. All species can roll into a ball to defend themselves. Even a mother carrying her baby on her tail will, when faced with danger, simply roll the young one up inside her. They can erect their overlapping scales, made from keratin (like human hair and nails) and shut them like powerful scissors, chopping off anything that pokes between

ANT TRAP

Lies on top of ant nest and opens scales

Ants swarm into gaps

Snaps scales shut to trap ants

Unfurls in pond and sucks up drowned ants from the surface

them, including fingers. The scales are, inevitably, a challenge when mating. Pangolins lie side by side, entwining their tails and forelimbs, so the male can slide in to one side of the tail. As for giving birth, happily the scales don't harden until several days later.

There is something mysterious about pangolins, beyond their surprising genetic provenance. Among the Lele people of northern Democratic Republic of the Congo, they are the inspiration for a fertility cult: scaly like a fish but able to climb trees; shaped like a lizard but suckling their young; and giving birth, like humans (usually) but few other animals, to just one offspring at a time. Ironically, it is this very strangeness that most threatens their survival, since across Africa and Asia they are eaten as ritual food, and their scales and body parts are used for adornment and traditional medicine.

Parrot
Vivid conversationalist

Parrots are probably the best-known birds in the world. After cats, dogs and rabbits, budgerigars (which are a kind of parrot) are the world's most popular pets. Almost all parrots are brightly coloured and they have names to match: Rainbow lorikeet, Purple-crowned lorikeet, Red-rumped parrot, Blue-crowned hanging-parrot, Sulphur-crested cockatoo, Peach-faced lovebird, Blue-and-yellow macaw. The colours in their feathers result from completely different molecules from those of any other colours in nature. Most parrots are green and males and females are almost identical in colour, but whereas male Eclectus parrots are

Parrots are an ancient group, which split off from the other bird families very early on. The oldest parrot fossil is 55 million years old, found in Walton-on-the-Naze in Essex, England.

bright green with scarlet underwings, the females are bright red with violet-blue breasts. For many years they were thought to be different species. Eclectus parrots are also the only species where the female is more colourful than the male.

Other unique parrots include two New Zealand varieties: the Kea (*Nestor notabilis*), or Mountain parrot, which is large and strong enough to mount the back of a sheep and tear out the fat round its kidneys while it's still alive, and the nocturnal Kakapo (*Strigops habroptilus*, or 'sensitive-eyed owl') the world's heaviest parrot and the only one that cannot fly. The world's smallest parrot, the Buff-faced pygmy parrot (*Micropsitta pusio*), is just over 3 inches long and the largest, the Hyacinth macaw (*Anodorhynchus hyacinthinus*), stands more than 3 feet tall. Most birds can move only one half of their beaks but parrots can move both. Their beaks are incredibly strong and close with a force of 350 lb per square inch but they have just 400 taste buds. This is a tiny number compared to people (who have 10,000) or cows, which, for some unknown reason, have about 25,000, but it's a lot for a bird. Parrots are among the very few birds that show any interest in sweet things. (Hummingbirds also like sweetness, but have only a tenth as many taste buds – between forty and sixty).

Parrots make loud, discordant shrieks, squawks and screams: very few have anything that could reasonably be described as a 'song', but the ancient Romans discovered they could speak and taught them to say 'Hail Caesar'. At first, talking parrots (imported from India) cost more than human slaves but eventually they became so common that the Romans got bored with listening to them and took to eating them instead.

No one knows how parrots get their remarkable ability to talk. No parrot in the wild has ever been observed to mimic the call of another bird or animal. In captivity, however,

THE LOVE BOOM

The male kakapo makes a mating court on top of a mountain, consisting of several carefully prepared 'bowls' connected by a series of tracks

He emits low-frequency 'booms' from them for up to four months to attract a female, losing half his body weight in the process

Puffed up air sac

they readily copy any commonly heard sound (such as doors slamming or car horns) as well as speech. Women and children are better at teaching them to talk than men, and African Greys, the least colourful of parrots, are the best pupils, able to mimic human speech perfectly. With the help of Dr Irene Pepperberg, Alex, an African Grey (*Psittacus erithacus*) bought in a Chicago pet shop in 1977, now speaks 200 words and fifty sentences. African Greys go on adding vocabulary throughout their lives and can live to be eighty years old. In 1800, the German naturalist Alexander von Humboldt encountered an elderly Amazon parrot in South America that could speak forty words of Ature, a language whose human speakers had long since died out.

Pearl Oyster
Nature's jeweller

You are very unlikely to find a pearl in your plate of restaurant oysters. Despite the confusing use of the name, edible oysters are about as closely related to pearl oysters as humans are to marmosets. Both are bivalves, anchoring themselves to rock in shallow seas and filtering algae from the current, but they are from entirely different orders and only one produces pearls of commercial size and value. Pearl oysters, close cousins to the scallop, live in tropical seas and can grow to the size of a dinner plate.

Another widespread misconception is that pearls are formed when a grain of sand or grit becomes trapped inside the oyster's shell. If that were true, pearls would be commonplace rather than highly valued rarities. The oysters' world is full of grit; they inhabit a universe of sand, and they spend their lives constantly ingesting and expelling it, with no trouble. Pearls are triggered by more serious intruders. These might be small bits of debris – pieces of bone, shell or coral, for instance – but in most cases it is something more purposeful. Oysters are troubled by various parasites, including species of worms, sponges and mussels, which drill through the mollusc's shell. This is the kind of major irritation which triggers pearl formation.

Having been invaded, the oyster acts to isolate the parasite inside a 'pearl sac'. The whole of the inside of its shell is covered by an organ called the mantle, which secretes mother-of-pearl. Also known as nacre, this is a wonder substance, strong yet flexible and lustrous, made by sandwiching calcium carbonate crystals between layers of an organic secretion similar to keratin. It entombs the enemy alien in successive coatings and the end result is a pearl. Pearl

> *Jeweller Pierre Cartier acquired his Fifth Avenue flagship store in 1917 for $100 plus a natural pearl necklace valued at $1 million ($15 million in today's money).*

MORE LIKE US THAN MOST PEOPLE THINK

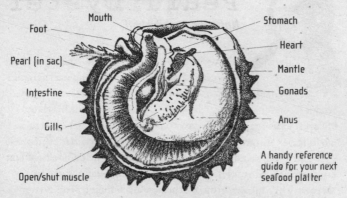

Foot — Mouth — Stomach

Pearl (in sac) — Heart

Mantle

Intestine — Gonads

Anus

Gills

A handy reference guide for your next seafood platter

Open/shut muscle

oysters can manage up to four layers per day but to create a layer of nacre a twentieth of an inch deep takes two years; a finished pearl, fifteen to twenty. That's why a ton of oysters might yield as few as three pearls, and the chances of them being perfectly spherical are, literally, one in a million. A single oyster might get several goes; in the wild they can live for eighty years.

The rarity and beauty of pearls led to many theories about their origin: that they were the result of dewdrops falling into the oyster while it sunned itself at dawn; or they were gallstones or crystallised angels' tears; or came from bolts of lightning. The 'grain of sand' idea was first posited in seventeenth-century Italy, while in the nineteenth century marine scientists proposed dead oyster eggs. It wasn't until the first decade of the twentieth century that French and Japanese researchers identified the pearl sac theory, leading to the first artificially cultured pearls.

Most modern pearls are farmed; it is a big global business with an annual turnover of over £300 million. It is a slow process. Each animal is opened and has a bead of mussel shell and a piece of mantle (cut from a 'donor' oyster) carefully inserted into its gonad. As the mantle fuses with the surrounding tissue, it is stimulated into producing a pearl sac, coating the bead with nacre. Two years later you get something that is indistinguishable from a natural pearl — just don't scratch it too hard.

Penguin
Black-and-white belly

Two-thirds of all the birds in Antarctica are penguins. The largest is the Emperor penguin (*Aptenodytes forsteri*, meaning 'wingless diver'), which can grow to a height of 3' 11", dive 1,700 feet deep and hold its breath for fifteen minutes. Forty million years ago there was a much larger Antarctic species, *Anthropornis nordenskjoeldi*, which was 5' 7" tall – the same height as Eddie Izzard or Michelle Pfeiffer. Emperor penguins are famous for their dogged dedication as parents. They take it in turns to look after their egg in bitter subzero weather, making epic trips to find food and losing 40 per cent of their body-weight in the process. Despite this, only 19 per cent of Emperor penguin chicks survive their first year. This must put a strain on the relationship.

It's often said that Emperor penguins mate for life, but in fact nothing could be further from the truth. While faithful for the breeding season and when the chick is being reared, at other times Emperor penguins have much lower rates of fidelity than smaller species. At least 85 per cent of Emperor penguins cheat on their partners. They're mostly straight, though, unlike Roy and Silo, two Chinstrap penguins at New York's Central Park Zoo, who hit the news when they built a nest together, rejected any advances from females and raised an egg. Silo eventually left Roy to pair up with a female named

UNGH!

GUANO GUN

Nest

Guano (viscosity of olive oil)

PAF!

Adélie penguins keep their nests and feathers clean when excreting guano by standing on the stony rim of their nests, leaning forward slightly and squirting. They can generate rectal pressure that is four times that of a human – about 7 psi (the same as a keg of lager). This propels it 16 inches away from the nest wall.

Scrappy and may well be the first documented case of an ex-gay or bisexual penguin.

By no means all penguins live on icebergs. Fiordland crested penguins from New Zealand nest in coastal rain forests; Galapagos penguins in tropical volcanic caves; Fairy penguins in burrows; and the Humboldt penguins of Chile in guano, piles of ancient bird droppings. Many penguins spend 75 per cent of their lives at sea. Only Emperor and Adélie penguins live exclusively in the Antarctic. Adélie penguins (*Pygoscelis adeliae*) are named after a French explorer, Jules Sébastien César Dumont D'Urville (1790–1842). In 1840, his ship reached an island off the Antarctic ice shelf, which his men named D'Urville Island in his honour. Later, they came across a little, fat penguin with a black coat and a white apron and named it after his wife, Adélie. The Adélie penguin lives in vast communities of up to 750,000 birds. Like other penguins, they have a manoeuvre called a 'slender walk', in which they pin their flippers back when squeezing through crowds. Female Adélie penguins build their nests with stones, a rare commodity in Antarctica and one for which they are willing to pay. When their partner's back is turned, they trade 'intimate favours' with other single males in return for bigger, better stones – the only known example of bird prostitution. 'Client' males are sometimes so satisfied with the service that females can come back for more stones without offering sex, merely a little light courtship. One particularly flirtatious female managed to acquire sixty-two rocks in this way. The males clearly believe the loss of stones is worth it for the opportunity to father more chicks. Zoologists speculate that the female may be trying to improve the genetic variability of her offspring.

Or she could just be having fun.

> *Penguins have much denser feathers than most birds, more than seventy per square inch, to keep them waterproof. Their black-and-white colouring is designed (like fish) to blend in with the sea when looked at from either above or below.*

Pig
More equal than others

There are about a billion pigs in the world and more than half of them live in China. The Chinese relationship with the pig is a long one: it was one of the places where the wild boar (*Sus scrofa*) was first domesticated, over 9,000 years ago, and to the Chinese 'meat' still means 'pork'. Pork is now the world's most popular meat: 85 billion tons are consumed annually, a third more than beef or chicken. Traditionally, its popularity has been related to the thick protective coating of fat that made it ideal for curing (the process of salting, drying or smoking which preserves the meat by preventing the fat from oxidising). In the last decade, health concerns have led to a halving of the fat content, the extra weight mostly being replaced by water. As well as food, dead pigs are a rich source of medical products such as insulin, their skin makes high-quality leather and their bristles are used in paintbrushes.

Throughout this long history of usefulness, humans have had an ambiguous relationship with the pig. To be a 'pig' implies gluttony, stubbornness and a lack of attention to personal hygiene. At the same time, we admire them for their intelligence and pluck. They are gregarious, playful animals and, as a result, are harder to herd than sheep or cattle: if a pig can escape, it will. Pigs eat both plants and meat, which makes them invaluable as re-cyclers of human food waste. But pigs don't eat 'like pigs'. They have a third more taste buds than we do (they don't like lemon rind or raw onions) and unlike sheep, horses (or humans) rarely overeat.

Pig stem cells are being used to research human diseases. In order to track them once injected, Chinese geneticists have crossed a pig with a jellyfish to produce piglets whose tongues and trotters glow fluorescent green in ultraviolet light.

However, their 'dustbin' status, which made them the backyard animal of choice for Asian and European peasants, also cemented their reputation as an 'unclean' animal, forbidden for Jews, Muslims and Seventh Day Adventists.

In terms of cleanliness, pigs are actually very particular. They are the only farm animals that make a separate sleeping den (which they keep spotless) and use a latrine area. They just don't look clean. They turn the ground more efficiently than any plough, 'rooting' incessantly with their snouts. This, combined with rain, quickly leads to mud. But pigs don't 'sweat like pigs'. Because they have no sweat glands, suffer from sunburn and carry a thick insulating layer of fat, they need a mud wallow to keep them cool and protected.

Pigs are highly intelligent. Like dogs they can be easily housebroken, taught to fetch, and come to heel. Pigs can learn to dance, race, pull carts and sniff out land-mines. They can even be taught to play video games, pushing the joystick with their snouts, something that even chimps struggle to master. In the eighteenth and nineteenth centuries 'learned pigs', dressed in natty waistcoats, amazed audiences with tricks. Pigs have even put on trial and hanged for murder. Maybe it's this intelligence that some people find unsettling. When a pig fixes you with its long-lashed, forward-facing eyes, and sniffs you with its snout (which is 2,000 times more sensitive than a human nose), a connection is made that goes well beyond the food chain.

THE PIG ORGAN

boar
bass

sow
alto

weaner
soprano

In 1450, the future King Louis XI of France commissioned the abbot of Baigne to put on an entertainment bringing together his two great enthusiasms: music and pigs. The resulting instrument was a huge success – the audience recognised the tunes

Pigeon
Undervalued visionary

Before we dismiss pigeons as 'rats with wings', consider why the rock dove, *Columba livia*, which originally appeared in Australasia twenty-five million years ago and which still lives happily on some sea cliffs, made such a complete transition to city life. Why are there so many? Cities are full of artificial cliffs (we call them 'tall buildings') and people throwing out stale bread and dropping half-eaten kebabs. Unfortunately, food stimulates breeding, with the result that we now have non-stop breeding pigeons, with some females laying six times a year, and raising as many as twelve squabs each.

Rock doves were first domesticated by the ancient Egyptians for food and message-carrying. Urban populations were established by escaped domestic birds and they've never looked back. The estimate for the damage caused by pigeon droppings in the US alone is $1.1 billion. But we shouldn't overreact: there is little evidence to suggest that pigeons pose a serious health risk to humans. The worst disease associated with them is psittacosis, or parrot fever. New York City, home to 100,000 pigeons, records one case per year and pigeons have proved particularly resistant to the H5N1 avian flu virus.

Pigeon eyes have split focus: the top half sees at great distances, the bottom sees detail close-up

According to the seventeenth-century natural historian John Aubrey, the traditional remedy for the bite of an adder was to apply the 'fundament of a pigeon' to the wound to suck out the poison.

Rather we should marvel at their gifts. To stay alive in the wild a pigeon needs to keep its eyes open for predators. Their position on either side of its head gives it a field of view approaching 340° and in order to fly at speed it has to process visual information three times faster than a human. If a pigeon watched a feature film, twenty-four frames per second would appear to it like a slide presentation. They would need at least seventy-five frames per second to create the illusion of movement on screen (this is why pigeons seem to leave it until the very last second to fly out of the way of an oncoming car: it appears much less fast to them).

The US navy has tried to exploit their keen-sightedness by training them to spot sailors lost at sea: they can pick out a far-away orange life-raft much better than a human. They have also been put to work inspecting drug capsules for defects. Pigeon vision is smart as well as sharp: they can tell the difference between Cubist works by Picasso and Impressionist canvases by Monet and are even able to tell when the Monets are hung upside down.

WHY BOB?
Because a pigeon can't move its eyes, it thrusts its head forward when walking, to keep it stable and maintain life-preserving visual focus

They also navigate with great precision, using a combination of odour trails, the sun's position, the earth's magnetic field and, as they get closer to home, visual landmarks like road systems.

Pigeons mate for life; widowed birds accept new mates very slowly. They are also model parents: the male and female take turns to incubate eggs, and care for their young in the nest. Both produce 'pigeon milk' in their crops. It isn't real milk – there is no lactose in it – but looks like cottage cheese and is fed to the chicks for their first ten days. That's why you don't see baby pigeons: they grow so quickly that by the time they leave the nest, they are almost the size of an adult.

Platypus
Electric otter

When George Shaw made the first written description of the platypus (*Ornithorhynchus anatinus*) in 1799, he first carefully checked the specimen he had been sent from Australia for signs of stitching. Even so, many of his naturalist colleagues continued to believe it was a hoax: a duck's bill sewn on to the body of a small beaver. It took thirty years for it to be accepted as a mammal — the lack of nipples made it difficult to locate the mammary glands under its stomach fur. But it wasn't until 1884 that the real bombshell fell. A Scottish embryologist called W. H. Caldwell finally uncovered a platypus nest and revealed the astonishing news that here was a mammal that laid eggs (the Aborigines had been saying this for years, but no one had listened). The platypus has remained notorious ever since, ridiculed as evolution's little joke.

A popular nineteenth-century view, still held in some quarters, describes the platypus as a crude early prototype of the mammal, subsequently abandoned. It is true that together with the four species of egg-laying echidnas it sits in the monotreme ('one-holed') order, the oldest surviving group of mammals. But to disparage it as a primitive, 'halfway house' between reptiles and mammals makes no more sense than calling a craftsman who builds wooden furniture from scratch more 'primitive' than someone who puts up flat-pack shelving from Ikea. The platypus is a perfect example of a creature that has, in isolation, adapted itself to exploit a rich habitat. Think of it as Australia's otter, an opportunistic carnivore, guzzling down freshwater crayfish, shrimps, fish and tadpoles with little competition. It has kept some of the 'reptilian' features, like egg-laying and a lizard-like way of walking, because there was no pressure to change them. But it has also evolved other new adaptations of astonishing sophistication.

The most ingenious of these is the 'duck's bill' itself. The platypus is a nocturnal creature, feeding at night and dozing in its burrow or 'wedging' under a rock or tree root by day. Hunting at night under water poses a challenge, as smell and sight are useless. The platypus's solution – unique among mammals – is to borrow a trick from fish and turn its 'nose' into an electrical probe. The bill is covered in 40,000 sensors that can pick up the tiniest electrical fields generated by muscle impulses in its prey. As well as that, it also has 60,000 motion sensors, allowing it to act as both eye and hand, with mechanical and electrical information combining to create a vivid picture of its dark underwater world.

It has also come up with its own dual-purpose propulsion system. As with beavers, the tail is used to store fat, but when the platypus swims, it acts as a rudder not a propeller. All the power comes from the large webbed front limbs. On land, these skin flaps fold away so it can use its front claws to burrow. Though as fast as an otter in water, the platypus rivals the mole as a digger of tunnels on land, which is why it earned it the name 'watermole' among the early settlers. Duck, mole, otter? Perhaps it's the mark of a true original that it can only be described in terms borrowed from something else.

BILL BRAINED

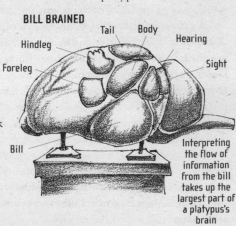

Tail　Body　Hearing　Sight　Hindleg　Foreleg　Bill

Interpreting the flow of information from the bill takes up the largest part of a platypus's brain

Porcupine
Raunchy and rhythmic

'Porcupine' literally means 'spiny pig', although they are rodents and not remotely related to either pigs or hedgehogs. There are twenty-five species, split between Old and New Worlds. All are spiny, but some New World species can climb trees and swing from branches using their tails like spider monkeys. In Europe, they are native only to Italy and Greece but have been known in Britain since 1110, when Henry I was given one as a pet.

The inevitable question that crops up with porcupines concerns their love life. As it turns out, avoiding the spines is the least remarkable detail. Porcupine sex often begins with both male and female walking on their hind legs astride sticks, which they use to stimulate their genitals. Once whipped up into a frenzy they stand belly to belly. With his now erect penis, the male soaks the female from head to toe with urine (streams reaching more than 6 feet have been recorded) and begins to make a loud squeaking, similar to the 'love song' of mice. The female turns her back on him and arches her tail over her back. There aren't any quills underneath it and he has no quills on his belly. The

> **Never rub bottoms with a porcupine.**
> **GHANAIAN PROVERB**

actual mating lasts only a minute but the male porcupine has a secret weapon. As with other rodents, his penis points backwards in its sheath, unfolds like a penknife when erect, and has bristly barbs on its tip. But the porcupine also has two pointy 'nails' on the underside that aren't found in any other animal. Whether they are for 'latching on', or giving added pleasure, we don't know.

The outcome, after a long gestation, is called a porcupette. Unusually for a rodent, there is only one. It is born with its eyes wide open and a fully developed set of quills, which are ready to use within twenty minutes. Indian porcupines (*Hystrix indica*) seem quite happy with the set-up.

American porcupines are strict vegetarians and suffer from low salt levels as a result – to compensate, they consume anything human sweat has touched: bags, trainers, paddles, garden furniture, etc.

They mate for life, and are the only rodents that copulate even when there is no possibility of conception, a helpful adaptation for the monogamous.

The scientific name for the Old World porcupines comes from the Greek word for them, *Hystrix*, while the North American porcupine's Latin name, *Erethizon dorsatum*, translates literally as 'I have a back that provokes'. Despite Pliny the Elder's assertions, they can't fire their quills, but tiny erector muscles in the skin do make them stand up. Then they lunge backwards, swiping their tails violently. Even tigers run scared.

There can be over 30,000 quills on a single animal, and they grow replacements. The quills are covered in backward-pointing scales. These help the quill to work slowly into flesh where it can be fatal if it hits a vital organ. To remove a quill, cut off the end sticking out first to equalise air pressure inside the wound.

Native Americans used porcupine quills to create sacred designs. The Arapaho no longer practise the craft because the last of the seven women who fully understood the designs died in the 1930s. To attempt quillwork without the proper ritual knowledge is considered dangerous.

African porcupines are attracted by loud drumming and can be taught to shuffle in time to the beat. Porcupine is still eaten there and in Italy, where they have a reputation for yielding even crispier crackling than pork.

Quoll
The Australian killer pussycat

The five species of quoll are known as 'marsupial cats', although they aren't remotely related to the felines. They don't look much like them either: their snouts are longer, more like a mongoose's or a ferret's, and they have spotted coats and long bushy tails (their family name *Dasyurus* means 'hairy tail'). But they fill the cat-shaped hole in the marsupial world, surviving as nocturnal, solitary predators with the most powerful bite for their size of any animal except their closest relative, the legendary Tasmanian Devil (*Sarcophilus laniarius*).

'Just wait till your father gets home . . .'

This killer streak even surfaces during sex. The female Northern quolls (*Dasyurus hallucatus*) all come into season at the same time each winter, leading to a free-for-all, as males try to mate with as many females as possible. Grabbing the female's neck in razor-sharp jaws, they drag them off for an average mating session of three hours, and sometimes for as long as twenty-four. It takes this long because they don't produce many sperm and need to ejaculate repeatedly to ensure conception. There's a lot of screeching and biting, as the females crouch with their eyes closed thinking of the spring, but many get injured, and some are even killed and partially eaten by their mate.

Female quolls carry their young dangling underneath them, even when climbing trees. When they are larger, they switch to their mother's back

In the case of the Northern quolls, at least, they get their own back. The males often don't recover from the exertion of the rut. They lose weight, become anaemic, their scrotum shrinks, their fur falls out and they get infested with lice. Within a week or two they die, martyrs to their genes. This reduces competition for food, giving the females and their offspring a better chance of survival, but also avoids the risk of incest the following season.

'Hungry?'

The Northern quoll is the smallest of the five and although it's not much larger than a guinea pig, it is fearless, taking on rats, snakes, lizards and pretty much anything that crosses its path. Unfortunately, this includes the poisonous cane toad (see above), which has encroached on its territories, and which it eats before it realises the danger. The population decline is now so steep that conservationists and local Aboriginal groups in the Northern Territories have transported small groups of Northern quolls to outlying toad-free islands.

All the Australian quoll species are threatened, both by introduced predators and by their own adaptive shortcomings. A recent test with the Eastern quoll (*Dasyurus viverrinus*) demonstrated that it couldn't tell the difference between the call of a fox and that of a cow. It is now only found on Tasmania and, although it regularly pops out thirty young, only the first six to find a nipple survive.

Even the Spotted-tailed or Tiger quoll (*Dasyurus maculatus*), the largest carnivore on mainland Australia, has been added to the endangered list, as its population has shrunk to fewer than a thousand. Its version of the quoll 'suicide gene' is to site its communal dung-heap in the middle of bush roads.

> The word 'quoll' was first recorded by Captain Cook in 1770. It comes from dhigal in the Guugu Yimidhirr language of Northern Queensland, which he transcribed as Je-Quoll.

In 2001, Michael Archer, director of Sydney's Australian Museum, suggested that to save quolls from extinction, people ought to take them up as pets: 'Instead of canoodling with dogs and cats, cuddle a quoll instead!'

Rabbit
The unstoppable pet-pest

'The introduction of a few rabbits could do little harm and might provide a touch of home, in addition to a spot of hunting.' Rarely has a human prediction proved more wrong. These were the words of Thomas Austin, an English settler in Australia who released twenty-four rabbits on his farm in 1859. Ten years later, there were so many across Australia that even a cull of two million made no dent in the population. By 1950, when the myxomatosis virus was introduced as a biological control, there were over one billion Aussie rabbits, the fastest spread of mammals ever recorded. As a result, an eighth of all native Australian mammals and an unquantifiable number of plant species perished, their habitats destroyed by overgrazing and erosion. Myxomatosis worked – the rabbit population was decimated, but the small number that survived have bred a genetic resistance to the disease, so a new, less effective virus (rabbit haemorrhagic disease) was introduced in 1995. The population is currently a hundred million and growing.

WORLD'S 3rd MOST POPULAR PET

There are over a hundred breeds of domestic rabbit in every shape, colour and size. All of them are bred from the European wild rabbit

Flemish Giant (20 lb)

Netherland Dwarf (1 lb)

What makes the European rabbit (*Oryctolagus cuniculus*) so successful? Firstly, diet. They will eat most things that grow, and in quantity: a single rabbit can eat enough grass to stuff a decent-sized pillow every day. Secondly, unlike hares and most other rabbit species, they run a communal burrow system which supports a large number of breeding females. And finally, they breed like – well – rabbits. A doe is usually either pregnant, lactating or both at once; she can produce thirty kits a year and they are all able to reproduce within six months of being born. Males tend to disperse to new colonies, females stay put to breed until the warren gets too crowded. Unless predation or disease intervenes, rabbit populations spiral.

Despite appearances, rabbits aren't rodents, they are lago-morphs ('hare-shaped'), one of over fifty species, including hares, pikas, jackrabbits and cottontails. Lagomorphs have a special trick: eating their food twice. Whereas a cow chews the cud, they eat their own droppings. Not the dry fibrous spheres we find scattered outside their burrows, but the contents of their large intestine, which look like bunches of shiny green grapes and are full of bacteria, generating essential nutrients, especially B vitamins. Strictly speaking, despite their provenance, these are not faeces, but food. They are coated with rubbery mucus to protect them from the digestive process and rabbits eat them directly from their bottoms.

It wasn't until the mid-nineteenth century that the resourceful rabbit became a serious agricultural problem in Britain. When they were first introduced by the Normans, rabbits were a valuable farm animal, kept in enclosed warrens (by warreners) for their meat and fur. Poaching rabbits was a high crime carrying draconian punishment. But by the 1820s, not only were landowners 'enclosing' their land with endless miles of hedges (the perfect environment for escaped rabbits), they also unleashed an orgy of shooting, poisoning and trapping of the foxes, martens, stoats and birds of prey that had previously controlled rabbit numbers. Ironically, the 'spot of hunting' that Thomas Austin fancied on his new Australian farm transformed the rabbits back home from crop to pest. The once exotic rabbit now costs British agriculture £100 million each year. Ironically, rabbit meat sold for the British table is mostly factory-farmed and imported from China, Hungary and Poland.

> *The Sumatran striped rabbit (Nesolagus netscheri) is so rare and shy that there is no word for it in the language used where it lives. It was thought extinct in the 1930s, and has only been seen three times since.*

Raccoon
Porky New Yorker

You can learn a lot about raccoons from the words for them in other languages. The English 'raccoon' is derived from Algonquian Indian *arahkoonem*: 'they rub, scrub, scratch.' In Dakota-Sioux, a raccoon is *weekah tegalega*, 'magic one with painted face'. In Abnaki, it's *asban*, 'one who lifts up things'. The Delaware Indians called it *wtakalinch*, 'very clever with its fingers'. Spanish colonists adapted the Aztec word *mapache* ('that which has hands'), although the Aztecs also called it *eeyahmahtohn* ('the little old lady who knows things').

Raccoons are the best-known wild animals in North America. They have a black mask over their eyes and a bushy tail with between four and ten black rings. They have five toes on each foot and their front paws are provided with thumbs, thanks to which they can lift latches, unscrew jars, disentangle knots, turn doorknobs and open refrigerators. Their paw-prints look like tiny human baby handprints.

Raccoon is a popular dish in the southern United States, the centrepiece for a traditional 'coon dinner'. Once the gamey fat has been removed, it is excellent roasted with a stuffing of sweet potato.

Raccoons adapt remarkably easily to the human environment and many of them live happily in New York City. They can live to be sixteen in the countryside but urban raccoons eat a similar diet to teenagers, becoming so dependent on French fries and doughnuts that they can't survive in the wild.

Fat is a raccoon issue: for some, 50 per cent of their body mass is fat. The fattest-ever raccoon was called Bandit; he lived outside Ice Cream World in Walnutport, Pennsylvania, and loved to feast on peanut butter and blueberry slush puppies. Raccoons are rightly called omnivores. They really will eat anything. They tuck into crayfish, apples, mice, eggs, insects, walnuts, frogs, fish, sweetcorn, clams, cherries, turtles, acorns, snakes and even road kill. Almost all non-American languages, from German and Finnish to Chinese, Japanese and Bulgarian, call them 'washing bears' because they seem to wash their food before eating it. For a long time, scientists thought this was because they couldn't produce enough saliva to swallow anything dry. In fact, this is not so. They have plenty of saliva, and they're not actually washing what they're about to eat. They do dunk food in water – an odd behaviour called 'dabbling' – but it appears they're just sorting out what is edible and not too sharp to ingest. If there's no water about they will still exhibit similar 'dabbling' behaviour and they're quite happy to eat food that has dirt on it. In search of food, raccoons are good climbers. They can rotate their back feet through 180° and climb head-first down trees, but they are equally at home in chimneys, haylofts and attics.

Raccoon droppings are crumbly, tubular and flat-ended. DO NOT EAT THEM. DO NOT EVEN TOUCH THEM. They may contain up to 250,000 eggs of *Baylisascaris procyonis*, a nematode worm that can cause severe illness in humans. If you eat the eggs, the larvae can migrate to other tissues, including the brain and eyes. There is no effective therapy. Raccoons look cute but many of them also carry rabies (of which they show no sign). They have bones in their penises (which people in Texas like to carry around for good luck). Dante Gabriel Rossetti, the Pre-Raphaelite poet, kept a raccoon in his Chelsea menagerie. It inspired no poetry, but did manage to disgrace itself by opening and eating its way through a whole drawerful of his manuscripts.

HANDSIGHT

Not many animals can safely take on a crayfish in the dark

Raccoons' hands are incredibly sensitive and are used more than sight and smell to locate and assess quality of food

Rat
Man's new best friend

Outside the polar ice-caps, the only place in the world where you won't find any brown rats (*Rattus norvegicus*) is the province of Alberta in Canada. From its home base in Mongolia, the brown rat followed the spread of human cities across the steppes, finally swimming the Volga into western Europe in 1727. From there it travelled the world on ships, scurrying ashore at every port and eventually reaching Alberta's eastern border in 1942. The Albertans decided to fight and set up a 400-mile-long buffer zone that is still patrolled by rat vigilantes. Alberta is cold and human habitation is sparse, so they may just hang on. For the rest of us, the battle was lost before it began. In the USA there are an estimated 150 million brown rats; in the UK, they now outnumber people.

> Some people say that you are never more than 6 feet away from a rat but actually I believe the distance is more likely to be about 70 feet.
> TONY STEPHENS, Rentokil

Here's the problem. A rat can swim for seventy-two hours non-stop. It can jump down 50 feet without injury. It can squeeze through a half-inch gap, leap 3 feet, climb vertical surfaces and walk along ropes. It can survive longer than a camel without water. It will eat anything that's edible and lots of thing that aren't (lead sheeting, soft concrete, brick, wood and aluminium). It reaches sexual maturity at three months. Rats have sex up to twenty times a day, and are extremely promiscuous: an on-heat female can have sex over 500 times with a barnload of different males and produce twelve litters of twenty-two young each year. In short, rats are very, very hard to get rid of.

Which would be fine if we could just grow to love them. That's the next problem. Brown rats consume about a fifth of the food produced in the world each year. They carry over seventy extremely infectious and unpleasant diseases: bubonic plague, of course, which has killed a billion, but also cholera, typhus, tuberculosis, Weil's disease, salmonella, cryptosporidiosis, E. coli, foot-and-mouth, SARS and eight species of parasitic worm. A quarter of all electrical cable faults are due to rats' ever-growing teeth, as are most 'unexplained' domestic fires. Like mice, their communication system involves near-constant urination – rats piss on one another to show affection, attraction, dominance and submission, and on food just to show it's edible. Oh, and they carry a lively subculture of fleas, mites and lice everywhere they go, which is everywhere we go. It is very, very hard to love the brown rat.

Not that there isn't plenty to admire. They are intelligent and resourceful, they learn fast and have excellent memories. Their sense of smell is of such sensitivity and refinement that it makes you wonder why they waste it all on water sports. They seem to have a sense of fun and an ultrasound giggle which they use when being tickled, during sex or when a rat they fancy sprays on them. They make very good pets, and despite the evidence to the contrary, spend almost half their lives keeping themselves clean.

But it doesn't matter what we think. Thanks to our wasteful habits, rats are unbeatable evolutionary winners. Maybe in time the brown rat will itself be driven out, as it drove out the black rat (*Rattus rattus*), which in the UK at least could now apply for endangered species status. But whatever takes its place, you can rest assured that it will only be a bigger, better, smarter rat.

FIRST CATCH YOUR RAT . . .

Rats are considered a delicacy in Africa and South-East Asia. Cantonese recipes include: crispy fried rat, braised rat with black pepper, salt-roasted rat and rat kebab

When catching a rat, it may jump up at you but it's not going for your throat: it's aiming for the daylight above your shoulder

Salamander
How to grow new eyes

The 500 species of amphibious salamanders come in every shape and size, from the giant Chinese (*Andrias davidianus*) which can be 6 feet long and weigh 5 stones, to the tiny *Thorius*, which is the smallest land-living vertebrate at half an inch long, and the smallest animal of any kind with proper eyes.

The axolotl (*Ambystoma mexicanum*) is the most celebrated. Only found in a single lake in Mexico, at a certain point in their evolution they just stopped developing into adults, and now spend almost their whole life in the water as large tadpoles. Why they took this backward step isn't clear. It might have been provoked by the land habitat around their lake becoming more hostile, but it doesn't seem to bother other salamander species that live there. Occasionally, they do grow up into something resembling an adult tiger salamander and this can be artificially stimulated by injecting them with hormones. 99 per cent of the world's axolotls are now kept in captivity, most of them descended from the six specimens that arrived in French zoologist, Auguste

THE MOST POWERFUL MUSCLE IN THE WORLD

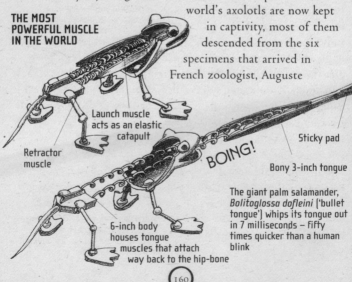

Launch muscle acts as an elastic catapult

Retractor muscle

Sticky pad

BOING!

Bony 3-inch tongue

6-inch body houses tongue muscles that attach way back to the hip-bone

The giant palm salamander, *Bolitoglossa dofleini* ('bullet tongue') whips its tongue out in 7 milliseconds — fifty times quicker than a human blink

Duméril's Parisian lab in 1863.

Salamanders are committed homebodies, travelling less than a mile from their birthplace over the course of their lives. This can prove fatal when the temperature changes: huge numbers perish each winter.

One species has beaten this problem. The Siberian salamander (*Hynobius keyserlingii*) can survive in temperatures as low as −50°C by producing anti-freeze chemicals before it hibernates.

They can stay frozen for many years – some may even have been slumbering since the last ice age ended, 10,000 years ago.

The most persistent myth about salamanders is that they live in fire and can douse flames with secretions from their skin (asbestos was originally called 'salamander wool'). No one knows where or why this idea arose, but they do have a dangerous habit of sleeping in damp woodpiles . . .

Newts are salamanders that return to the water to breed. They are the only vertebrates that can regenerate large parts of themselves, growing new limbs, spinal cords, hearts, jaws, tails and even new lenses and irises for their eyes.

Newt cells can restart the growth process. As the damaged part heals, the cells reverse their original function and turn back into an undifferentiated lump called a *blastema* (from the Greek *blastos*, bud) from which the replacement limb or tissue grows. If a blastema is moved to another part of the salamander's anatomy, the missing bit will start growing there.

How the cells know what to grow isn't understood, but salamanders are being studied closely to see whether human tissue could be stimulated to regenerate. Also, because malignant tumours seem to grow in a very similar way – injecting cancerous tissue into newts can also cause a new limb to grow – they may hold important clues in the fight against cancer.

Scorpion
Fluorescent assassin

Scorpions were the first predators to crawl out of the sea on to the land, and they have evolved very little in the last 430 million years because they are very good at what they do. In their prime, during the oxygen-rich atmosphere of the Carboniferous period, scorpions as big as dogs roamed the land, and in the sea giant water scorpions grew to twice that size. Like their younger arachnid cousins, the spiders, scorpions are tough and adaptable, putting up with sub-zero temperatures and desert heat. They can even survive two days completely submerged in water. They are found on all major land masses except Greenland and Antarctica. For 200 years, an illegal immigrant colony of yellow-tailed scorpions (*Euscorpius flavicaudis*) has lived in the harbour wall at Sheerness in Kent.

Isidore of Seville believed that scorpions were formed from the dead bodies of crabs and, though very fond of the smell of basil, will never sting the palm of your hand.

Part of this indestructibility is due to their highly efficient metabolism. They eat slowly but for several hours at a time, dissolving their prey with powerful stomach juices, and leaving behind a small ball of indigestible tissue. A single meal can increase their weight by a third, and some species can survive on that for a year, storing their food as glucose in a large liver-like organ. They burn energy at a quarter of the speed of insects and spiders and very few scorpions ever need to drink. This gives them an advantage as predators but they are also very well equipped when they do need to kill. They have two sets of eyes: one to tell them the time of day or night and a more complex set, with lenses and retinas, that are the most light-sensitive organs of any invertebrate. Using the hairs on their claws they can triangulate the precise position of lunch, picking up vibrations caused by movements as slight as 25 millionths of an inch.

Unusually for an arthropod, a female scorpion gives birth to live young. Even more extraordinarily, some species are pregnant for longer than humans. They are one of the very few invertebrates to have independently evolved a womb where embryos are fed by teats linked to the mother (rather than by the yolk of an egg). Labour can take days, with up to a hundred offspring scurrying up their mother's claws to nestle on her back underneath her sting, so nothing can get to them. Nothing that is except the mother, who, if suddenly peckish, may snack on them herself.

Despite the widespread myth, scorpions do not go mad and sting themselves to death when a drop of alcohol is placed on them, or when confronted with fire, as they are immune to their own venom. Of the 1,500 known species of scorpion, only twenty-five have stings that are dangerous to humans; most are no worse than a bee sting. Scorpion venom can even save lives: protein from the Israeli yellow scorpion's (*Leiurus quinquestriatus*) venom has been used to kill brain tumours.

Scorpions are fluorescent under ultraviolet light as a result of special proteins in their exoskeletons. As they can't see this themselves, no one is quite sure why. It might be to mimic insect-attracting plants, to warn off predators or even to act as an in-built sunscreen.

DIRTY DANCING: SCORPION 'FOREPLAY'

1. He stings her to get her in the mood

3. Claws lock

4. They dance until she's in the right position to 'lock and load' and receive the parcel's lively contents

2. He combs ground flat and deposits sperm parcel here

Sea Cow
Slow and seductive

The sea cow family, or sirenians, contains the dugong (*Dugong dugon*) and three species of manatee (*Trichechus*, after their 'hairy' snouts). As their common name suggests, these large, docile creatures are the only aquatic mammals that live on plants. Although they look like grey tuskless walruses, their closest relatives aren't cows, walruses or whales but another large herbivore, the elephant.

Sea cows have a very laid-back life. They paddle around in warm tropical seas, with little competition for food and no natural predators. As a result, they have a very leisurely metabolism. The largest adults weigh over a ton and spend eight hours a day slowly chomping through six straw bales' worth of aquatic plants, which take a week or more to digest. Life is slow enough for algae and barnacles to grow on their skin. Some dugongs have been recorded as living into their seventies, and they only manage one calf every three to seven years.

> Manatees often congregate near power plants, because of the warm water. In return, they keep the surrounding channels clear of weeds.

When they aren't eating or sleeping, sea cows come together regularly to 'cavort'. These sessions of nuzzling, bumping, kissing and mutual masturbation are often male-on-male, but can involve up to four individuals of either sex and last for several hours. The normally silent manatees make a sequence of distinctive 'snort-chirps' as they cavort, though no one knows how (even if we can guess at why). This pleasure-filled life, combined with the female dugong's large and elaborate clitoris and pendulous 'breasts', has contributed significantly to the mermaid myth. In the Solomon Islands, 'dugong' is the slang term for prostitute.

Dugongs and manatees also have a reputation for stupidity and their brains are, proportionally, small and smooth, roughly the equivalent of our brains shrunk to the size of a plum. In their defence, their brains seem well up to the job and some have even been trained to recognise colours and patterns in return for food.

More significantly, low metabolism and the absence of stress help make them impervious to the diseases which afflict other mammals, propelling them to the forefront of research into cancer and HIV.

This may also explain why they have six neck vertebrae rather than seven. In mammals, the genes that specify the number of vertebrae also control the nervous system and cell growth. Changes in this genetic data can cause cancer, so natural selection has tended to leave them alone. However, in a low-metabolism mammal like a sea cow the risk of cancer is greatly reduced. Over time, this might have allowed the genes to risk variation. Interestingly, the only other mammal with an irregular number of neck vertebrae is the sloth, another noted slacker.

'Manatee' comes via Spanish from a Carib word meaning 'breast', while 'dugong' derives from Malay 'duyung' meaning 'lady of the sea'. Like elephants, they have two teats under their forelimbs, causing sailors to mistake them for mermaids.

'Hello, sailors!'

But there is a downside. Slow, inquisitive and delicious (roast dugong tastes like veal) is a bad combination when faced with *Homo sapiens*. All four sea cow species are now endangered, as result of hunting, pollution and damage from propellers and fishing nets. The historical precedent is grim. Their relative, the Steller's Sea Cow, three times the size of the largest manatee, was hunted to extinction in the twenty-seven years after its discovery in 1741.

Sea Cucumber
Streetsweeper of the deep

Sea cucumbers have been trundling along the bottom of all the planet's oceans for 500 million years. They do an essential job as marine binmen, processing over 90 per cent of all the dead plant and animal material that settles on the sea floor. Many of them do look like knobbly cucumbers. Their family name, *Holothuridae*, is thought by some to mean 'completely disgusting'. The Romans called them *phallus marinus*, presumably because of their shape, and even Darwin dismissed them as 'slimy and disgusting'. One Mexican species, *Holothuria mexicana*, is known as the Donkey dung: a perfectly accurate, if unflattering, description.

THE INNER CUKE

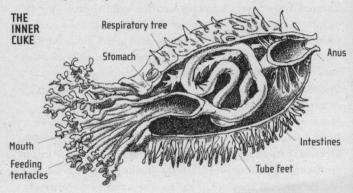

Respiratory tree

Stomach

Anus

Mouth

Feeding tentacles

Intestines

Tube feet

Despite their shape, the 1,100 species of sea cucumber are close relatives of the starfish and the sea urchin, sharing the same fivefold body symmetry and, like them, moving on tube feet driven by piped seawater. But 'cukes', as marine biologists call them, have other tricks. They breathe through their bottoms, drawing in water through their anus to fill a respiratory 'tree' and then expelling it along with any digestive waste that might be lurking. Single hole: two functions. This fact has been exploited by the tiny eel-like pearlfish. They wait until the cucumber's anus opens in the morning and then sneak inside, spending a leisurely day swimming around the intestines, before emerging again to feed at night. Some even knock to gain entry. Juvenile pearlfish are less welcome as they have a habit of gnawing on the cucumber's gonads.

Cukes are nocturnal and need to fill their guts at least twice a night, so life mostly alternates between sand-vacuuming and resting. If they are stressed or threatened, they have an impressive array of escape strategies. Their bodies are made from a connective tissue called 'catch collagen', which gives them an almost miraculous ability to change from solid to fluid. This enables them to 'pour' into the tiniest crevices and then stiffen again so they can't be extracted. Some species can blow themselves up to the size of a football. Others expel water to make themselves look like pebbles, but the ultimate cucumber party-trick is to blow their guts out of their bottom and flood the surrounding water with a toxic soup. Known as a 'cuke nuke', this can wipe out all the fish in a small aquarium, as well as the cucumber itself.

Some species have a more sophisticated version, expelling fine sticky threads, known as Cuvierian tubules, out of their backsides. These form an astonishingly sticky net which can tie up a hungry crab for hours. On the Pacific island of Palau, islanders milk cucumbers of their tubules and bind their feet with them to make improvised reef shoes. They are also used as a sterile dressing for wounds. Amazingly, a cucumber that has been harvested of its guts, gonads or tubules can grow them back within a couple of months.

Dried sea cucumber, known as *trepang* or *bêche-de-mer*, is eaten as a delicacy all over Asia, and has a reputation as both an aphrodisiac and a painkiller. The global sea cucumber market has grown to £2.3 billion and this is putting pressure on some species, leading to the establishment of cucumber farms and sea 'ranches'.

Seal

The grizzly submarine

Don't be fooled by their cute looks: the seals' closest relatives are bears and they can be every bit as vicious. One of the ways you can tell if a Leopard seal (*Hydrurga leptonyx*) is in the area is an empty penguin skin floating on the water. They violently shake the hapless bird from side to side to remove its coat and then gulp down the naked corpse. They are almost as bad with their loved ones. The male Southern elephant seal (*Mirounga leonina*), six times larger than his partner, occasionally gets carried away during copulation and accidentally crushes her skull between his massive jaws. And when female Hawaiian monk seals (*Monachus schauinslandi*) come into heat they risk being 'mobbed', which is the polite scientific term for being battered to death by a gang of amorous males. In order to save the species from extinction, males are now being put on libido-suppressing drugs.

> 'Selkies', the legendary Scottish seal women who leave their skins behind and are tricked into marriage by humans, may be a dim folk memory of visits by shaman from Lapland, who dressed in skins and used healing magic. 'Seal' is a Saami word.

With elephant seals, and their close relatives, the sea lions, this male aggression is also backed by huge size. The bigger and more aggressive the male, the bigger his bit of breeding beach and the higher the number of females he gets to service. A single male might have up to fifty females in his harem, but some harems grow as large as a thousand, serviced by just thirty males, with the top five – the 'beachmasters' – getting most of the action.

Much of the inter-male violence is just noise – loud gargling and slaps – but when fights do break out they can be bloody for both the participants and innocent bystanders. The females don't help: they make such a racket during mating that every male in the area makes a beeline towards them. In the resulting melee, pups get separated from their mothers, and are crushed or flung out of the way. Some colonies lose two-thirds of the pups in a single season in this way. It is one of the reasons seals' milk has the highest fat content of any mammal's: to ensure the pups grow quickly. The milk is more of a pudding; at 60 per cent fat it's twice as rich as whipping cream. Unsurprisingly, pups put on several pounds a day and are weaned within a few weeks.

It is in the sea that the seal's strength and aggression really sets it apart. A seal hunting in water is twice as efficient as a lion on land. Elephant seals can dive for two hours at a time and reach depths of 5,000 feet. They expel all the air from their lungs to avoid the risk of 'the bends' and survive on the oxygen absorbed in their blood. Their bodies hold twice as much blood as most mammals and, when diving, their heart rate plummets from ninety to just four beats a minute. To help them sink faster, some will even swallow stones.

Better still, a seal's eyes don't go blurry underwater. In other mammals, this blur is caused by the outer lens (cornea) being rendered useless by the water, like a transparent glass marble which disappears when you drop it in the bath. Seals overcome this through a huge spherical inner lens to focus the image, and an extremely adjustable iris to control the light. This not only gives them their big-eyed charm, it also means they can hunt in bright sunlight and the gloomy ocean depths.

HOW TO TELL A SEAL FROM A SEA LION

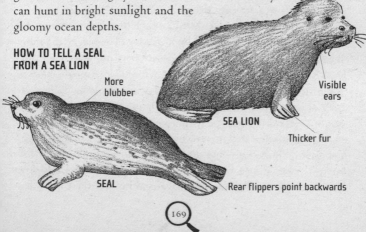

More blubber

Visible ears

SEA LION

Thicker fur

SEAL

Rear flippers point backwards

Shark
Big girl's blouse

Only one in a hundred shark species attacks people. In 2005, there were just fifty-eight shark attacks reported worldwide. Only four people were killed. Wasps kill as many people in Britain every year and jellyfish in the Philippines ten times as many. In the US, both dogs and alligators kill more people than sharks. To put it another way, in an average year in New York there are 1,600 cases of people biting people. Sharks have far more reason to be scared of us. We kill at least 70 million a year for food (despite the fact that some shark flesh tastes of urine, both 'rock salmon' and 'huss' are sharks) and for their livers (which are used in haemorrhoid cream).

It's a good job sharks find people a bit on the bony side and prefer seals. They are armed with a terrifying range of surveillance equipment. Two-thirds of a shark's brain is dedicated to smell: it can detect blood diluted in water at strengths of one part in a million and from a distance of a quarter of a mile. Nor does lunch have to be bleeding for the shark to know it's there. Shoaling fish exude chemicals to warn colleagues when danger threatens. Sharks intercept these signals, scenting fish that are not even wounded, merely nervous. A shark's ability to detect low-frequency sounds means it can hear the very heartbeats of fish from far away, and pressure-sensitive receptors along its body allow it to 'feel' the remote movements of prey through the water. Cells under the skin of its head enable it to pinpoint tiny changes in magnetic fields and minute electrical impulses. These not only help it to navigate as if using a compass, but provide yet another killing aid: sensing individual muscle movements of a distant fish even

> *If you turn a shark upside down it will go into a trance-like state called 'tonic immobility' for fifteen minutes. No one knows what causes it.*

when buried under sand. Some sharks even have a depth gauge in their middle ear. Equipped with this sophisticated gear, predatory sharks are able to hunt in total darkness.

Although in daylight they have perfectly good eyesight, these night raids must be their undoing. Items found in sharks' stomachs include beer bottles, bags of potatoes, a tom-tom drum, car number-plates, house bricks, a suit of armour and a whole porcupine. A single tiger shark was found to have swallowed three overcoats and a raincoat, some trousers, a pair of shoes, a driving licence, a set of antlers, twelve intact lobsters and a whole hen-house full of partly digested chickens.

The female frilled shark holds the world record for the longest pregnancy in nature: over three years. The largest egg in nature belongs not to the ostrich but to the female whale shark. Discovered in 1953, it was 12 inches long, 6 inches wide and 4 inches thick. The embryos of female sand tiger sharks kill and eat each other in the womb. But since records began in 1580, fewer than 2,500 shark attacks on humans have been reported. This is equivalent to about 6 per cent of the number of Americans injured by lavatories in 1996 (43,687).

Male sharks do not have penises. Which probably explains a lot.

RADIOHEAD

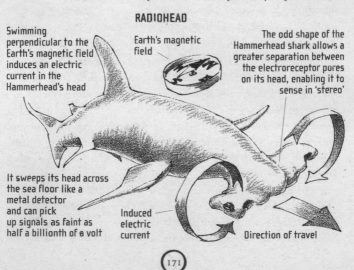

Swimming perpendicular to the Earth's magnetic field induces an electric current in the Hammerhead's head

Earth's magnetic field

The odd shape of the Hammerhead shark allows a greater separation between the electroreceptor pores on its head, enabling it to sense in 'stereo'

It sweeps its head across the sea floor like a metal detector and can pick up signals as faint as half a billionth of a volt

Induced electric current

Direction of travel

Sheep
A thank-you note

Domesticated sheep (*Ovis aries*) may only exist because of humans – but we, in our modern form, only exist because of sheep. First domesticated in the Middle East and Central Asia around 9000 BC, some time after dogs, reindeer and goats, all modern sheep can trace their lineage back to two ancestral breeds, one probably extinct, the other, the tiny – and now endangered – mouflon (*Ovis musimon*). Sheep, even more than their close relatives the goats, were responsible for the greatest lifestyle shift in human history, the transition from hunter-gathering to farming. Goats were perfect for nomads, but sheep, because of their tendency to flock and their ability to graze on the toughest grass, allowed us to stay in one place. Sheep fertilised the ground they grazed on, allowing agriculture to flourish, and their flesh and milk gave us a break from hunting. To get the best out of sheep, they needed to be herded and guarded, leading to larger human settlements (and more work for the recently domesticated dog). Interestingly, the Latin for sheep, *ovis,* and the English *ewe* both derive from the Sanskrit *avi,* which has its roots in *av* meaning 'to guard or protect'. Looking after sheep gave us civilisation.

It took 3,000 years for our ancestors to discover that by selectively breeding sheep they could encourage their fluffy

SHEEP THAT STAND OUT IN A FLOCK

Outlier
Goes off on its own, usually because it's weak and hungry

Bellwether
Sheep wearing a bell, that other sheep follow – often a castrated ram

Riggwelter
Sheep that has fallen on its back and is too heavy to get up

Soay sheep from St Kilda, were isolated for 4,000 years and reverted to a feral state. They have to be peeled, not shorn, and stare in blank incomprehension at sheepdogs. All you need to keep them is a pair of binoculars.

undercoat to grow longer than the bristly guard hairs (called 'kemp'). The result was first felt and then wool, and suddenly humans had yarn, then looms and textiles. If sheep farming was the first industry, wool became the first great trade commodity. By the Middle Ages, wool drove the economies of Europe: the Renaissance was largely financed on the profits from the wool trade. Today, synthetic fibres have dramatically reduced wool production in Europe and America: 60 per cent now comes from Australia, New Zealand and China.

Perhaps this apparent readiness to offer themselves up for our benefit has fed into their cultural role, which, historically, has been all about sacrifice. Unlike the more sexually suggestive associations attached to the goat, sheep have invariably found themselves being offered up in thanks, or having to symbolise innocent victimhood. The sacred texts of Judaism, Christianity and Islam overflow with lambs, flocks and shepherds. More recently, sheep have become a byword for conformism and stupidity, which is not only ungrateful but wrong. Far from being dim, sheep have good memories: they can recognise faces of other flock members and the face of their shepherd for up to two years. This facility has long been known by hill farmers, whose flocks have become 'hefted' to a particular territory. Shepherds and dogs initially teach them which ridges, boulders and streams mark the grazing boundaries. The ewes then teach this to lambs and it gets passed on from generation to generation, sometimes stretching back hundreds of years. The loss of 'hefted' flocks was one of the hidden costs of the 2001 outbreak of foot-and-mouth disease, in which seven million British sheep were slaughtered. More recently, super-smart sheep have learned how to cross cattle-grids by taking a good run-up and then rolling up in a ball to cross them, SAS-style.

Snake
Happy eater

No one is born with a fear of snakes: it has to be learned. Even then it's not really rational. In Florida, which is home to more than seventy different types of snake, 500 times as many people are bitten by dogs and far more people die from both bee stings and lightning strikes than from snakebites. The chance of being hurt in a road accident in Florida is at least a hundred times higher than that of being bitten by a snake. Snakes are not aggressive and do not chase after people. Even if they did, you'd just walk away. A rattlesnake travels at a top speed of 2 mph. The fastest snake ever recorded, a black mamba (*Dendroaspis polylepis*, 'many-scaled wood snake'), clocked up only 10 mph.

The smallest known snake is the burrowing thread snake (*Leptotyphlops bilineata*, 'double-lined skinny blind-eye'). It is 6 inches long and as thin as a matchstick. No one knows how large the largest snakes are because the really big ones have never been brought back to be measured scientifically. At the beginning of the twentieth century, a reticulated python on the island of Celebes was said to be 33 feet long, and a green anaconda in Colombia reportedly measured 37.5 feet. No snakes as long as these have been reported for a hundred years. Snakeskin is so valuable that no snake survives long enough to grow to that size.

> Snakes have two penises hidden inside their bottoms. The one on the right is often larger, suggesting that they are 'right-penised' in the same way most humans are right-handed.

The lips of boas and pythons are the most sensitive heat-detectors in nature. They can sense temperature differences of a 1000th of a degree between an object and its background and judge its direction and distance with similar accuracy. Such snakes find and kill their prey in total darkness by sensing their body heat alone. The heat-detectors of rattlesnakes and pit vipers are so acute that a deaf, blind snake that has had its tongue cut off can still accurately strike its prey. Many snakes can taste air and see heat.

There is no such thing as a vegetarian snake. Snakes eat nothing except other animals. Anacondas and pythons can open their mouths wide enough to swallow deer and goats whole and a python is easily a match for a leopard or a crocodile. Whether they get indigestion is not known, but the powerful acids in their stomach mean a snake will explode if given Alka Seltzer. Most snakes eat once a week; some only eight or ten times a year. After a big meal, a python can go for a whole year without eating and female adders don't eat for eighteen months.

Keen sunbathers, snakes, like many other animals that strike fear into people, do not like to be disturbed. When this happens, most of them wriggle away. The Sonoran coral snake (*Micruroides euryxanthus* 'yellow-banded small-tail') accompanies this with small, regular, high-pitched farts. Grass snakes (which are otherwise harmless) emit a disgusting stench of rotten garlic from their anal glands. They then vomit the contents of their stomachs all over the path. If that doesn't put you off, they flip over on to their backs and lie motionless with their mouths open and their tongues lolling out. Whether this is a defence mechanism or just bad acting is unknown. Most researchers never get close enough to ask them.

WHEN DINNER'S BIGGER THAN YOUR HEAD

Snake jaws don't dislocate: all the bones of the skulls are joined by elastic ligaments, allowing the mouth to open to 150°

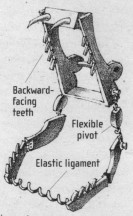

Backward-facing teeth

Flexible pivot

Elastic ligament

Lower jaws move independently of each other, alternately ratcheting or 'walking' prey into the throat

Spider
Worldwide webmaster

If spiders didn't exist, we'd have to invent them; without them, we'd simply drown in insects. Until the late eighteenth century, we just assumed they *were* wingless insects, but they now have their own class, *Arachnida*, which contains 40,000 identified species, with as many again waiting to be named. They were one of the earliest land animals to evolve and are predatory, territorial carnivores: put 10,000 spiders in a sealed room and you will eventually end up with a single fat spider. The mass of insects eaten by British spiders in a year outweighs the UK's human population. And by 'eat' we really mean drink: they dissolve their victims first.

That's an impressive trick, but not unique to spiders. What spiders do best is spin webs. Spider's silk is five times stronger than steel and thirty times more stretchy than nylon. It is so light that a strand long enough to circle the world would weigh the same as a bar of soap. It is made from protein strands and water spun together; the protein gives it strength, and the surface tension of the water lends it elasticity – but we still don't really understand how it's done. An average spider will spin more than 4 miles of silk in a lifetime, and this can be collected and woven into garments. However, their predatory nature makes them tricky to farm, so we will have to wait for genetic engineering to deliver spider-silk parachutes, bullet-proof vests and artificial tendons.

The tarantula's bite was supposed to bring on extraordinary symptoms: stupor, involuntary erections and an uncontrollable desire to dance off the venom in a violent and energetic dance (the 'Tarantella') for over three days. It turns out it was another spider's bite that brought on these symptoms.

Some spiders use their webs to fly. Called 'ballooning', it involves them climbing to the top of a fence, pointing their

whee!

backsides into the air, squirting out a long line of silk and letting the breeze take them. They can travel immense distances and have been found as high as 16,000 feet. Spiders can create perfect webs almost anywhere, even in zero-gravity, but give them drugs and they lose the plot. In 1995, a NASA experiment revealed that marijuana made them lose concentration halfway through spinning, whereas amphetamines made them spin quicker but much less accurately. Caffeine was the most extreme: the coffee web consisted of a few threads randomly strung together.

Male spiders don't have a penis. To mate they ooze drops of sperm on to a special sperm web. They then suck this up into one of a pair of specially adapted legs, called 'pedipalps'. The pedipalps insert, twist and lock it into the corresponding female slots and pump in the sperm, rather like R2D2 uploading into a mainframe. Often the end snaps off on completion. Inserting these pedipalps can be a perilous business for the male: his partner can be a hundred times his size. In one species, the Tent cobweb weaver (*Tidarren sysiphoides*), the male chews off one of his pedipalps beforehand to gain a speed and mobility advantage over the other suitors. He usually dies on the job, his dead body keeping his sperm safe from competitors for several hours. The male Australian redbacks (*Lactrodectus hasselti*) actually compete to be eaten. Being devoured by the female ensures that their pedipalp gets in first.

Although spiders are surrounded by fear and superstition, humans do sometimes eat them. The Piaroa people of Venezuela consider the world's largest spider, the Goliath bird-eating tarantula (*Theraphosa leblondi*), a delicacy. Roasted, they yield a quarter-pound of prawn-like white meat and are served with their fangs on the side, as toothpicks.

Despite their reputation, female black widows only eat one in ten of their mates, although they can get through twenty-five partners in a day

Starfish
No brain, clever feet

Starfish aren't fish; they are much older. The echinoderms ('spiny skins'), which also include sea urchins and sea cucumbers, first appeared in the early Cambrian period, about 550 million years ago, and haven't changed much since. Unlike molluscs and insects, they have an internal skeleton made from plates of calcium carbonate called *ossicles*. This makes them the direct relative of all vertebrates, including humans.

They don't have a central brain, but being star-shaped, they don't have a 'front' or 'back' either. The nearest they get is a ring of nerves that runs round their mouth. From this an individual nerve runs down each leg. As one leg moves – usually the one closest to food – it lets the others know to follow it. A splendid advantage to this system is that starfish can regenerate lost limbs, and in the case of the *Linckia* species, the lost limbs can even regenerate a new starfish. The early stages of this process – one large arm, a tiny body and four tiny arms – look like small seaborne comets.

Starfish have a mouth (underneath) and an anus (on top) but they arrived a long time before ears, eyes or noses. Instead, they have hundreds of multi-tasking tube-feet covering their underside. They use these to breathe, to move and to attach themselves to prey. They also function as noses, assisted by the skin's sensory cells (2.6 million per square inch), responding to chemical changes in the water around them, and locking on to 'odour plumes' given off by potential food. At the tips of the legs, 'eyespots' (which may be mutated feet) act as light sensors.

Starfish move using simple hydraulics. They take in seawater through a special sieve-like opening called a

Series of water-filled suckers propels starfish along surfaces

madreporite and distribute it internally to all the feet-tubes. By squeezing and sucking water in and out of the feet in sequence, they can move surprisingly quickly. Some species manage three feet a minute.

Starfish sex is a strictly arm's-length business. Each leg contains a large sex organ, but short of dissecting them it is impossible to tell male from female. They gather in groups when spawning, the male releases sperm into the water if he detects eggs; the female releases up to two and half million eggs at a time if she detects sperm. The larvae are completely unlike their parents and look more like free-swimming plankton. Eventually they grow arms, sink to the bottom and stick to a rock, before metamorphosing into adults.

> In business jargon, a 'starfish' organisation is completely de-centralised. On the other hand, passive sexual partners are sometimes described as starfish because they 'just lie there'.

Fully-grown starfish have few predators; their spiny skin is covered in tiny pincers which nip at anything that annoys them. They also 'groom' the skin, keeping it clear of parasites. One species, *Luidia*, just disintegrates into fragments if it gets caught.

Starfish eat almost anything too slow to escape, particularly mussels and oysters. A square-mile army of starfish was recently sighted off Le Morbihan in France, at a density of fourteen to the square foot, moving slowly across the ocean floor and consuming everything in its path.

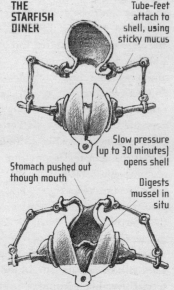

THE STARFISH DINER

Tube-feet attach to shell, using sticky mucus

Slow pressure (up to 30 minutes) opens shell

Stomach pushed out though mouth

Digests mussel in situ

Tapir
Ancient forest horse

When Stanley Kubrick cast tapirs alongside early hominids in the opening sequence of *2001: A Space Odyssey*, it was because they seemed 'prehistoric'. He was right: they may look like the result of a night of passion involving a pig and an anteater but tapirs are the last survivors of a large family of mammals that have changed little in twenty million years. At one point they were found on every continent (except Antarctica) but now there are only four species left: three in Central and South America and one on the other side of the world, in South-East Asia.

Tapirs are perfectly adapted to life in warm, wet forests. They can graze on the forest floor for fallen fruit and browse higher up for green twigs and ferns. Their stout bodies barrel through thick undergrowth at high speed and they are as happy in the water as on dry land. But the key to their early success remains their most distinctive feature, a short, multi-directional trunk – the ultimate accessory for forest life. It gave them greater reach when feeding, functioned as a snorkel for travelling under water, and provided a con-tinuous olfactory read-out on the presence of food, or the possibility of sex.

But the climate has changed, and cooler, drier conditions have seen forests replaced by grassland, which favours grazing ruminants, not short-sighted, semi-aquatic fruit-chewers. Unlike

Small eyes

FOURTEEN TOES AND ONE FINGER

Picks leaves and feeds itself with finger-cum-nose

Three toes on each back foot

Four toes on each front foot

their closest relatives, horses and rhinos, tapirs haven't managed this transition, and now all surviving species are endangered.

As well as the loss of habitat, tapirs are also threatened by human predation. Hundreds are poached each year for their fatty meat (often sold as buffalo), their durable hide (*tapira* is a Brazilian Indian word for 'thick') and the various parts of their anatomy still used as folk cures for heart disease and epilepsy. In many Amerindian tribes, the Milky Way is known as the 'Tapir's Way', in the same way the American Plains Indians call it the 'Path of the Buffalo'. In China and Japan, their name means 'dream-stealer'.

> *The Thai word for tapir is P'som-sett, which means 'mixture'. It comes from the belief that the tapir was made from the leftover bits of all the other animals.*

Other than humans, tapirs are too strong and nimble to have many predators. Occasionally, a big cat will take one on, in which case the tapir simply leaps into a nearby stream and sinks until the cat is forced to let go. Tapirs like walking on the bottom of streams and ponds: it cools them down and allows fish to strip their hide of parasites.

Tapir calves look very different from their parents: they are striped and spotted, like furry watermelons. This provides surprisingly good camouflage in the dappled shade of the forest, but they still fall prey to the giant anaconda, which likes to swallow them whole. Although we call their offspring 'calves', zoologists have now agreed that tapirs are sufficiently different from other hoofed mammals not to call the adults 'bulls' and 'cows'.

Tapirs are the least well-studied of all large mammals. We don't know whether they mate for life, how their family groups work, where they sleep, or the function of their strange bird-like whistles. But this is changing. Their importance in the ecosystem of the rainforest has made them a conservation landmark species. Just as they need the forest to survive, so many of the forest fruiting plants depend on the tapir's digestive tract to propagate. Saving the tapir will help save the rainforest, too.

Tardigrade
The bear that wouldn't die

Tardigrades are the toughest animals on the planet. Also known as 'water bears' and 'moss piglets', they sound cute, but don't be fooled. They live anywhere there's water — 5 miles down in the ocean; on the polar ice-caps; in radioactive hot springs; on top of the Himalayas; on forest floors; on the bottom of lakes; on wet beaches; in Alpine meadows; in the miniature ponds created in the cups of leaves; in the moss on your roof; on the ground where your dog pees each morning. They are plump, microscopic animals that fall somewhere between the annelid worms and the insects. Only a twentieth of an inch long, they have a head, four pairs of stubby, clawed legs and a sausage-shaped, opaque body. They're called water bears because of the way they look and move (although they're more like a section of frayed, rumpled leg-warmer) and moss piglets because moss is one of the best and easiest places to find them.

> A tardigrade in suspended animation is called a 'tun', because it looks a bit like a tiny wine barrel.

There are 800 recorded species of tardigrade, with at least 10,000 still to be named and they are distinctive enough to have

INSIDE THE RESURRECTION MACHINE

Cross section of self-fertilising tardigrade

Ovary

Gut

Brain

Nervous system (ganglia)

Sperm receptacle

Anus

Mouth

Throat (pharynx)

their own phyla. Most land-dwellers feed on plants and fungi, but many are carnivorous, sucking up nematode worms, rotifers and other tiny creatures. The water-dwellers (who can live 100,000 to the pint) seem to survive without eating at all for long periods, although some are parasites, living on sea cucumbers and barnacles. Many species are all female. As they aren't speedy at getting around ('tardigrade' means 'slow-stepper'), they rely on the wind or splashing raindrops to move them to new habitats. Under those circumstances, being able to fertilise your own eggs is a definite advantage: you can populate a new clump of moss all by yourself. Other species reproduce sexually, in a topsy-turvy kind of way (the female inserts a tube into the male and steals his sperm). Tardigrade eggs are spectacularly beautiful, shaped into multi-pointed stars and dimpled spheres that look like chic lampshades, although their practical function is to keep their contents moist and safe from being squashed.

What really sets tardigrades apart is their ability to enter a state of suspended animation. If their water supply dries out, they dry out too. All life processes come to a complete halt and they become totally inert – but they are not dead. This condition, known as cryptobiosis, was first identified in 1776. Some scientists believe it may hold the clue to the origins of life itself. The tardigrade expels all its water and breaks down its cell fats into a sugar called trelahose, which binds and protects all its vital organs. Then it waits – for as long as a hundred years – for a single drop of water to revive it.

In this 'dead' state, tardigrades are practically indestructible. They have been frozen to within a degree of absolute zero (−272 °C) and heated to temperatures of 151 °C. They have been placed in liquid helium for a week, and given doses of radiation a thousand times greater than the fatal dose for a human. They have been immersed in chemicals and squeezed by pressures six times greater than those at the bottom of the ocean; but like living granules of instant coffee, with one drop of water, back to life they come.

Termite
Family values

Termites have evolved the most sophisticated family organisation of any animal and it's based around monogamy. Despite living in colonies containing millions of individuals, breeding termites mate for life. Some species only have one king and queen per colony; others have several and, unlike those of ants or bees, these are proper marriages not brief flings: there are couples still mating years later. This has helped make termites, with ants, the most successful insects of all: if you added all 2,600 termite species together, they would account for 10 per cent of the planet's total biomass. Unfortunately their high-fibre diet means they also produce 11 per cent of global methane emissions, second only to ruminants like cows and sheep.

But life doesn't always run smoothly, even for termites. In the species *Zootermopsis nevadensis* the divorce rate is running at about 50 per cent. Sometimes the males walk out; often the female invites in a new male with predictably violent results. Touchingly, rejected termites tend to take up with one another. Marriage leaves the male termite relatively unaffected, although he usually dies first. The queen, however, can swell to 300 times her original size, as her ovaries expand. The queen of the Indian mound-building termite (*Odontotermes obesus*) lays an egg a second, or more than 80,000 a day. If the nest is attacked, the workers have to drag her to

HOW DOES YOUR WOOD SOUND?

Termites decide on which wood to eat by the vibrations it gives off when they start chewing

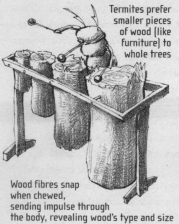

Termites prefer smaller pieces of wood (like furniture) to whole trees

Wood fibres snap when chewed, sending impulse through the body, revealing wood's type and size

safety, as she is too fat to move of her own accord.

To make things worse, termites are in the middle of an identity crisis. In 2007, DNA research revealed that they are actually cockroaches. Their former order *Isoptera* ('equal wing') has been abandoned and they have been moved into *Blattodea* (*blatta* is Greek for cockroach). The theory is that they evolved from their cockroach-like ancestors when they developed the ability to eat wood.

> Didgeridoos are made from eucalyptus logs hollowed out by termites.

It's the blind workers who do the wood-munching, feeding the rest of the colony from their mouths or bottoms. They are like mini-cows, with a multi-chambered stomach to break down cellulose. Their guts are home to 200 types of microbes which all help turn the wood into energy. Studies of these tiny organisms are being funded by the biofuel industry to see if they hold the key to extracting clean-burning fuel from corn. In some species, workers arrange their droppings into combs which grow fungi, ensuring a supply of rich protein, even during the dry season.

A termite nest is the most complex animal structure not built by us. The external mound can be over 25 feet high, protecting the nest from the fierce sun, acting as an air-conditioning duct by releasing the heat and carbon dioxide generated by the termites and their fungus gardens and replacing it with fresh oxygen. The Formosan subterranean termite (*Coptotermes formosanus*) even fumigates its nest with naphthalene to repel ants and nematode worms. As it doesn't occur naturally, no one knows how – or from what – it is made.

> Termites can burrow through concrete. In North America, they cause more damage than fires and floods put together; the annual global termite damage bill now exceeds $5 billion.

Termites are one of the most popular culinary insects: they contain 75 per cent more protein than rump steak. In the Amazon basin, the Maue tribe barbecue them while the Kayapo fry them in their own juices or use them crushed as a condiment. In Nigeria you can buy termite stock cubes.

Toad
When amphibians explode

Few animals spook us like the toad. The witch's right-hand animal, they have been feared throughout history as ugly, poisonous creatures of the night. Touching them might give you warts and meeting their stare could turn you epileptic.

In East Anglia, to become a 'toadman' was to make a pact with the Devil, the most dangerous initiation ritual of British folk magic: all your power was focused in the bone of a toad, which no one else was allowed to see or touch.

Wearing the legs torn from a toad guarded against skin disease. Carrying its tongue made you irresistible to women. Breast cancer could be cured by rubbing a live toad over your chest, and the best protection against witches was to bury a toad in a bottle near your door or hearth. Killing them was strictly taboo.

Despite all the bad press, toads, taxonomically speaking, are members of the frog family. There are 350 species and the main differences are skin and teeth. Frogs tend to have tiny teeth and smooth skin; toads have no teeth and thick, warty skin, and usually walk rather than hop.

'Toady' (as in 'sycophant') comes from 'toad-eater', one half of an eighteenth-century pair of con artists, who would swallow a toad in public and then beg his quack doctor-partner to cure him with a 'magical elixir'.

Also, unlike most frogs, toads are poisonous. They secrete a milky fluid from their warts and from a pair of glands behind their eyes — the 'toad spittle' of legend. In some species this venom contains hallucinogenic compounds and can be 'milked' for recreational use. Unfortunately, it also contains powerful steroids which cause irreparable damage to the heart. Licking or kissing toads is likely to make you sick long before it gets you high.

Twenty tons of toads are squashed

While I'm Away
1. Pick up kids
2. Twine around back legs
3. Wander about for 3 weeks
4. Dangle legs in pond until they swim off
5. Do it all again next year XX
PS Don't talk to crows

The male Midwife toad (*Alytes obstetricans*) fertilises several females – and then gets to carry the eggs himself

on British roads every year. This is because they have followed the same path, century after century, to ancient breeding ponds, which often means crossing busy roads. Purpose-built subterranean toad tunnels have helped, easing the passage of as many as 1,500 toads in a single evening.

'Toad-in-the-hole' was originally steak encased in batter, until steak became too expensive and was replaced by sausages. The name was taken from a now-forgotten public craze of the nineteenth century. Hundreds of examples were reported of live toads being discovered entombed in the middle of ancient rocks. 'Toad-in-the-hole' hysteria peaked in the 1830s when William Buckland, the Oxford Professor of Geology, buried a number of toads in stone blocks to test their survival skills. Although some lived for as long as two years, most died and public fascination waned.

A more recent toad mystery took place in a Hamburg pond in 2005, when toads started exploding during the mating season. More than a thousand toads, swollen to three times their usual size, crawled out of the water, making eerie screeching noises, and blew up, propelling their entrails up to a yard away.

Initial suspicions of a virus or industrial pollution turned out to be wrong. The toads were being attacked by super-smart crows. The birds had worked out that, with a single strike through the toad's chest, they could remove its liver. The toad's own defence mechanism did the rest. As they puffed themselves up to intimidate their attacker, they forced their own intestines out through the wound at high pressure, in a kind of fatal hernia.

Tuatara
Three-eyed loner

Most species described as 'living fossils' struggle to fully justify the claim but not the tuatara. This ancient reptile looks like an iguana, but it isn't a lizard. Nor is it a dinosaur, although it has changed little since the days of the giant reptiles. It's a *sphenodon*, or 'wedge tooth', the last member of an order that once covered the planet. The tuatara has survived for two reasons. Firstly, it happened to find itself on the small land mass that became New Zealand about eighty million years ago, as it split from Gondwanaland, the southern super-continent, before mammals had established themselves. And second, it found a way of adapting to a colder climate.

Most of the sphenodons disappeared with the dinosaurs; those that didn't got hustled out of their niches by mammals. The tuatara ploughed its own furrow quite happily for millions of years, until the mammals finally reached them, paddling canoes. With the canoe-mammals came others, most notably dogs and rats. The tuataras were gradually driven from the mainland and now survive only on islands dotted around New Zealand's coast.

Their main disadvantage in the battle with mammals is metabolism. Tuataras are the most primitive of all living reptiles. Their brain is tiny, more like an amphibian's than a lizard's. Their heart and circulatory system are also rudimentary, making them extremely cold-blooded, and they live on islands which are often wind-battered and chilly. Out of necessity, 'do it slowly' has become the tuatara's motto. They grow more slowly than any other reptile. It takes them fifteen years to reach sexual maturity and even then, the females only manage to produce a clutch of eggs every four years and they take

Tuatara means 'spiky back' in Maori. The Maori once ate them but only the men – a woman who broke the rule risked being pursued and killed by the entire tuatara population.

over a year to hatch. Their method of hunting is to sit outside their burrows at night waiting for beetles, worms, crickets, or — best of all — a young tuatara to toddle past. Their method of defence is to sit inside their burrow waiting for the danger to go away. That's no challenge for a sprightly rat. In 1981, the island of Whenuakura had a population of 200 tuataras. By 1984 they had gone, replaced by a colony of rats.

Several features set the tuatara apart from their lizard cousins. They can live for well over a hundred years. They don't have teeth but all-in-one serrated jawbones: in old tuataras these jaw 'teeth' are worn smooth, leaving them to gum their way through slugs and earthworms. Also, unlike the doubly endowed lizards, tuataras have no penis: they reproduce by pressing their bottoms together, like birds and (probably) dinosaurs.

Oddest of all is the third eye in the middle of their forehead. Although scales grow over it by the time they are six months old, it is a real eye with a lens, retina and a nerve connection to the brain. It appears to be light-sensitive and might help in regulating body temperature. Temperature matters to a tuatara: they live cheerfully in conditions that would trigger hibernation in most reptiles (10° C), so heat can kill them. Rising temperatures also pose a more serious threat. As with turtles and crocodiles, the sex of the hatchling is determined by the heat of the egg. The warmer northern colonies of the 55,000-strong tuatara population are now producing twice as many males as females.

3 Once it bites, haul it out — tuataras never let go

HOW TO CATCH A TUATARA

1 Find occupied burrow

2 Irritate occupant by dangling tennis ball on string

Walrus
A violent lunch companion

The word 'walrus' may be from Dutch *walros* ('shore-steed') and its Latin name *Odobenus rosmarus* means 'tooth-walking seahorse', but walruses look nothing like horses. They are almost as round as they are long; they have no visible ears and they drag themselves along by their teeth. They also change colour when heated, from off-white to pink to cinnamon brown. A beach heaving with basking walruses looks like a skip-load of deformed cocktail sausages.

Walruses are inordinately fond of seafood. They enjoy cockles and mussels, crabs, shrimp, snails and octopus and can wolf down more than 6,000 clams in a single meal. Clams bury themselves in the seabed, so the walrus first has to unearth them. To do this, it brushes the sediment away with a flipper and it almost always uses the right-hand one. There are no southpaw walruses. It was long assumed that all animals are ambidextrous, but recent research has shown this is not so. As well as walruses, whales, chickens and toads tend to lead with their right, whereas frogs and lizards favour the left.

> The walrus in Lewis Carroll's 1871 poem 'The Walrus and the Carpenter' was inspired by a stuffed specimen in Sunderland Museum, of which only the head remains. The poem, in turn, inspired John Lennon's acid anthem 'I Am the Walrus' on Magical Mystery Tour.

Another way that walruses feed is to create a high-pressure hose effect using their lips and tongues to blast the seabed and expose their lunch. This creates a thick murk of sand and debris, so, rather than using their small eyes to identify prey, they slide along feeling the bottom with their moustaches. These are composed of more than 400 incredibly sensitive whiskers, known as *vibrissae*, Latin for 'vibrators'. A grazing walrus can move each of them independently.

Walruses suck as well as blow. When they find a clam, they hold it firm in their lips, create a vacuum around it and use their tongue like a piston to extract the soft tissue. As a special treat, they hoover up seagulls from underneath or suck the brains of seal pups out through their nostrils, a party trick also used by young Inuit in Greenland to impress tourists. Walruses have a sucking power three times stronger than the average Dyson, which explains why their stomachs are full of small pebbles.

Medieval merchants used to pass off walrus tusks as unicorn horns. They are canine teeth that never stop growing; in a large male they can be 3 feet long. Apart from helping them haul themselves on to ice floes, they are mostly for show. Walrus society is simple: the bigger the male, the more impressive the tusks, the more lady walruses make themselves available.

Mating among walruses is much like a sub-zero version of a Club 18–30 holiday. The females lounge provocatively on the ice, while being ogled by a pack of alpha-males bobbing around in the water, trumping, clacking, roaring, rasping and occasionally gouging chunks out of one another. Unlike those in Club 18–30, however, the female will only mate with one male. Walrus sex takes place underwater and it's impressive stuff. The male's penis contains a bone almost as long as its tusks, which guarantees fail-safe operation in even the coldest Arctic seas.

THE ARCTIC SUPERMARKET

Walruses are a one-stop shop for the Inuit

Tusks for carving

Blubber for lamp oil

Skin for boats

Intestines for waterproofs

Penis bone for club

Meat for a thousand meals

Wasp
Sugar and paper

Of the thousands of species of wasp out there, there are only two that regularly bother us: the Common wasp (*Vespula vulgaris*) and the German wasp (*Vespula germanica*). There's not much to chose between them: both live in colonies and fashion delicate spherical paper nests, both have a nasty retractable sting, both cause a huge fuss at late summer picnics. Wasps, of course, suffer the great misfortune of not being bees: they don't make us honey, their markings are stark and uncuddly and their behaviour seems thuggish in comparison to the mystical dances and complex social life of their furry cousins. This is unfair; for a start, bees are really just vegetarian wasps. Each of them has a job to do and without the voracious appetite of the wasp many insect pests would overrun our gardens.

The appetite is not quite what it seems. Like bees, most of the wasps we see are sterile females, but in spite of their impressive mouthparts, they have a very simple digestive tract, which means they can only eat sweet nectar. They kill and scavenge tirelessly, but not for themselves. Their jaws are used to chew up protein for the endlessly hungry larvae back at the nest. Then, in return for bits of bacon sandwich or beetle, they get a blob of sweet, nutritious 'soup' from the larva's mouth. But at summer's end, this food source runs out. Its breeding work done, the commune disperses; next year's queens find a sheltered place to spend the winter, while everyone else gradually dies off. This is when worker wasps — now unemployed and unfed — become a nuisance to humans. In the last few, purposeless weeks of their lives, before cold weather finishes them off, they seek alternative sources of sugar, in our kitchens, orchards and picnics. It's now that most human–wasp interaction occurs — sometimes with fatal consequences, for wasp and human.

Often these interactions culminate in one of the humans

claiming they are being attacked by a 'hornet'. The hornet (*Vespa crabro*) is the largest and noisiest of the European social wasps, which no doubt explains why people have long been terrified of it. But, in fact, its sting has much less effect on humans than that of a bee. Bees have evolved their venom as a defence against honey-stealing vertebrates, including beasts the size of bears and badgers, whereas a hornet's poison is intended mainly for use on its invertebrate prey. Analysis of hornet venom suggests that a fatal dose for a human (unless he was allergic to it) would be something like a thousand stings.

> *It's a bad idea to kill a wasp: dying wasps emit a pheromone that alerts its nest-mates to danger, so you may be surrounded within seconds.*

There is an important exception. The Asian giant hornet (*Vespa mandarinia*) of Japan, also known as the yak-killer, is the super-predator of the wasp family. They are enormous – like flying thumbs, with a quarter-inch sting. They are fast, strong and merciless – ten of them can take out an entire honeybee colony in a matter of hours, tearing off the bees' heads with their terrifying jaws. Their venom is strong enough to dissolve human tissue and they kill over fifty people a year. But the Japanese get their own back in style: they serve the larvae raw as hornet *sashimi* and deep-fry the adults, which are reputed to taste like sweet prawns.

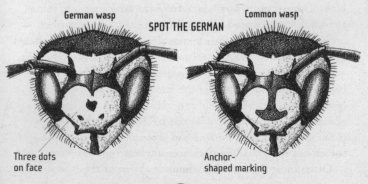

German wasp   **SPOT THE GERMAN**   Common wasp

Three dots on face

Anchor-shaped marking

Whale
Supersized songsmith

Fifty-five million years ago, small hoofed carnivores started to move from the land back into the sea. Those wonderful pictures of legs becoming fins and tails, bodies becoming longer and more streamlined, nostrils moving back and up, seem to run the evolutionary clock backwards. DNA evidence now shows us that whales have nothing to do with other water-based meat-eaters like seals and walruses; their closest living relative is the vegetarian hippo, with deer, camels and pigs as very distant cousins. It's one of evolution's most compelling stories: how a clumsy, crocodile-shaped otter ends up producing the largest, most graceful and mysterious of all the creatures on the planet.

> Blue whales were only caught after the invention of the 'grenade' harpoon in 1868. In 1931, 29,000 were killed in one season. There are now fewer than 5,000 – one whale for every 8,500 cubic miles of their ocean habitat.

The blue whale is the largest animal that has ever lived by a huge margin: thirty times heavier than an African elephant, the next largest mammal. The biggest dinosaur weighed less than half as much: some female blue whales can lose as much as 50 tons when feeding their young. A newborn blue whale is the same weight as a female elephant: it puts on 14 stone a day, 8 lb an hour. When fully grown, its heart is the same size as a family car, processing 2,000 gallons of blood, pumping 60 gallons a beat, with an aorta large enough for a five-year-old child to swim through.

Whales grew large because the buoyancy of water meant they could – nothing so heavy could survive on land; the energy needed to move and feed would be too great. But for a warm-blooded animal living in the sea is problematic: it's a desert – there's nothing to drink. And it's cold: heat travels twenty-four times faster in water. Being large helps, as it reduces the surface-

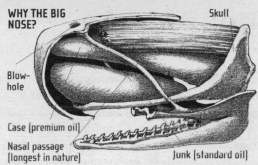

WHY THE BIG NOSE?

Skull

Blow-hole

Case (premium oil)

Nasal passage (longest in nature)

Junk (standard oil)

Sperm whales are one-third head. It houses a brain four times the size of a humans and 4 tons of 'spermaceti', once thought to be the whale's semen. Humans use it as transmission fluid, watch oil and fun putting the shine in lipstick. The whale uses it to talk

to-weight ratio, but the real star of whale survival is blubber. It not only acts as an insulating overcoat and life-jacket (it's less dense than seawater); it also stores the water extracted from food and provides a handy on-board supply of nutrients when food is scarce.

Communicating in water is also a challenge. Smell is useless, sight limited and touch is tricky when you have fins rather than fingers. But sound waves travel four times faster under water, and whales have turned the ocean itself into a sophisticated communication system. Whale song is the loudest noise made by any single animal: some songs are so low in frequency that they can be felt thousands of miles away. The massive head of the sperm whale focuses sound into a burst that can stun a giant squid but it also acts as a kind of acoustic retina, a giant IMAX sound screen through which it interprets its dark world. The half-hour songs of the humpback whale contain grammatical rules: sounds are combined into structures that operate like syntax, packing the song with millions of discrete units of information. Whales sing in different dialects depending on where they're from, and sing different songs in different places at different times of the year.

Whether these songs are sat-nav read-outs, shipping forecasts, personal ads or epic poetry, we will never know. What we do know is that military sonar and general noise pollution in the sea has reduced their carrying range by 80 per cent and many stranded whales have severe inner ear damage. We may not hunt whales as once we did, but we still torment them.

Woodlouse
The backyard shrimp

Woodlice are land-based crustaceans, and, despite appearances, are much more closely related to shrimps and lobsters than they are to millipedes or centipedes.

They have blue blood and still breathe using gills, These are attached to the pairs of *pleopods* (literally, 'swimming feet') on their abdomen and contain a branching network of moist tubes that allow them to extract oxygen from air, although a woodlouse will survive quite happily in water for up to an hour.

Woodlice have a rich array of nicknames: 'sow bugs', 'ball bugs', 'armadillo bugs', 'slaters', 'grammerzows', 'chiggy pigs', 'cheeselogs' 'bibble bugs', 'cud worms', 'coffin cutters', 'monkey peas', 'pea bugs', 'granny-ants', 'granfers', 'Billy Bakers' and 'tiggyhogs'. In Holland they are called *pissebed* (literally 'piss-in-the-bed'). This is because they don't urinate: their porous shell also allows them to expel their waste as ammonia vapour rather than liquid urine. They produce more nitrogenous waste for their size than any other animal.

The porous shell also means they are vulnerable to dehydration. Their tendency to clump together in large groups helps keep them moist and protects them from predators. Toads, shrews and centipedes are all keen on woodlice. Blowfly larvae also burrow into woodlice and eat them from the inside. The woodlouse spider (*Dysdera crocata*) lives on nothing else and has specially adapted fangs for piercing their shells.

Woodlice do use their bottoms to drink. Small forked tubes called

> Woodlice were eaten as a cure for stomach upsets, rather like Rennies – their shell is made from calcium carbonate, which neutralises the acid in the stomach.

uropods suck water into their anuses. They're not fussy eaters either. They prefer rotting vegetation, but in lean months their own faeces will do. There's a New Zealand species, the sea slater (*Scyphax ornatus*), that

Woodlice drink through their bottoms – the uropods can also ooze a noxious chemical gum to keep spiders away

survives mostly on drowned honeybees. Their odd personal habits make them good news in a compost heap and their fondness for munching through rubbish has led to them being employed by natural history museums to clean delicate animal skeletons.

Woodlice are members of the Isopod order (meaning 'equal feet'). There are 3,500 species and they've been around for 160 million years. They carry their young in pouches, moult regularly and live for about two years. Not all of them clump together in damp crevices. The desert woodlouse (*Hemilepistus reaumuri*) pairs for life, navigates by the sun and lives in organised colonies of burrows where the young do the housework. They can walk several miles a day.

It's tough being a male woodlouse. Not only can females give birth without mating (parthenogenesis), but males infected with a certain bacterium actually turn into females.

The Deep sea isopod (*Bathynomus giganteus*) is a giant aquatic woodlouse that lives on the icy darkness of the ocean floor and hoovers up dead whales. They are white, 2 feet long and weigh as much as a decent-sized lobster.

'First she goes and reproduces without me, then I catch an infection and turn female!'

'Lousy luck, mate ...'

Woodlice are perfectly edible. In his polemical pamphlet *Why Not Eat Insects?* (1885), Vincent M. Holt considered their flavour superior to shrimp and gave a recipe for a woodlouse sauce for fish.

Woodpecker
The tongue that listens

The woodpecker's tongue is one of the most amazing of all animal organs, so much so that it often gets cited by creationists as 'proof' that evolution is flawed. In some species it can extend to fully two-thirds of the bird's body length, is covered in sticky saliva, has vicious barbs and has an 'ear' at the end of it. In fact, tongue structure of the woodpecker is very similar to that of most other birds: it's just longer, presumably because this delivered the evolutionary advantage of being able to reach deeper into the tree for insects. The secret is a series of wafer-thin hyoid bones, that fold up like an accordion in a fluid-filled sheath when the tongue is not being used. As the woodpecker sticks out its tongue, powerful muscles contract near the base, forcing the bones forward and the tongue out of the bill. Relaxing the muscles brings it back inside. When a woodpecker is born, its tongue is anchored near its ears, much like a chicken's. As it grows, the hyoid sheath gradually extends around and over the skull, when it fuses with the back of the nostrils. As for the ear on the tongue's tip, this is a concentration of pressure-sensitive nerve endings called Herbst's corpuscles that feel the tiniest vibrations of insect prey.

> My father told me all about the birds and the bees, the liar. I went steady with a woodpecker till I was twenty-one.
>
> BOB HOPE

When not in use, the tongue squeezes up for storage around outside of skull, fixed to back of nostrils.

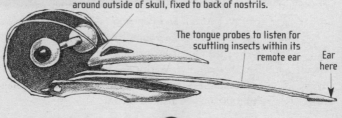

The tongue probes to listen for scuttling insects within its remote ear

Ear here

There are over 200 species of woodpecker, and each has a particular speed and rhythm of drilling, some reaching sixteen blows per second. Every time a wood-pecker brings its head to a halt, the force is equivalent to a thousand times the force of gravity (or 250 times the force an astronaut is subjected to during lift-off). The reason that their heads do not shatter is a sponge-like cartilage cushion that absorbs most of the shock. Also, every time the wood-pecker strikes a blow, a muscle pulls the brain-case away from the beak.

Muscles pull back the brain in sync with pecking to act as shock-absorber

POK!

Woodpecker drumming isn't searching for food. It's a species 'signature' used to communicate and attract mates. Woodpeckers often choose materials where the resonance is high – dead trees, metal drainpipes or wooden caves. They drum at different rates when insect-hunting or excavating nests. In 1995, a pair of Northern Flickers (*Colaptes auratus*) drilled 200 holes into the foam insulation of the shuttle *Discovery*'s external tank, delaying its launch.

Green woodpeckers (*Picus viridis*) are also known as rainbirds – hearing their distinctive 'laughing' call means rain is on its way. This dates back to an early version of the Genesis story, where the woodpecker refused to help God excavate the rivers and oceans and was punished by being forced to peck wood and drink rain. The bird once had forty English vernacular names including Hewhole, Wudewale and Galley Bird, but the one still used is 'Yaffle'. Most people assume this refers to its laugh but it actually means 'to eat greedily'. Which green woodpeckers do, as anyone who's ever seen one attacking an anthill will testify. They can get through 2,000 ants in a single sitting.

Worm
Wiggly woo woo

The animal kingdom is subdivided into thirty-four categories called phyla. There is some disagreement among biologists about the precise number and placing of the divisions, but everyone agrees that more than half of them (usually seventeen) are made up of various kinds of worm. There may be more species of beetle, but there are more individual worms in the world than any other type of creature. No matter how many cattle there are in a field, the worms under the soil will always outweigh the cows on top of it.

Nematodes, or roundworms, are parasitic worms found almost everywhere on earth from the ocean floor to the human gut. They are the most numerous animals on the planet, ranging from a hundredth of an inch to 27 feet long. There are about 40,000,000,000,000,000,000,000,000,000,000,000,000,000,000,000,000,000,000 nematodes all told and their DNA is 75 per cent identical with that of human beings. Most nematodes are benevolent, humbly servicing the ecosystem, but some are dangerous parasites that can cause river blindness, elephantiasis and hookworm anaemia. Then there are flatworms and segmented worms, spoon worms and peanut worms, ribbon worms and horsehair worms. Velvet worms live in old leaves and rotting logs. They paralyse animals and liquidise them with saliva. Acorn worms live in U-shaped burrows on the seabed. They eat and excrete mud. Those little coils you see on the beach at low tide are acorn worm droppings. All worms except paddle-worms are hermaphrodites. *Pseudoceros bifurcens* is a flatworm that lives 60 feet underwater in Queensland, Australia. It performs a mating dance called 'penis-fencing'. The worms spend up to an hour trying to inject each other with sperm: whoever wins gets to be the male. Ribbon worms will eat their own bodies if their food supply runs out. They can eat up to 95 per cent of themselves and still survive.

Lewis Carroll said he liked worms 'because nobody else does' but Charles Darwin was also a huge admirer. He spent days counting earthworms in his garden while his son played the bassoon to them. There are 3,000 species of earthworm, ranging from 2 inches to 11 feet long. Good soil contains a million earthworms per acre. A typical earthworm has no lungs, teeth or eyes but it has ten hearts, arranged in five pairs. Though they are eyeless, their skin detects changes in light.

> It may be doubted whether there are any other animals which have played so important a part in the history of the world, as have these lowly creatures.
> **CHARLES DARWIN**

Their simple brains are used merely to tell their bodies how to react to these changes. If you removed an earthworm's brain, you wouldn't notice much change in its behaviour. The sex organs of an earthworm are located in the clitellum, the bulge a third of the way from the front of the worm that looks like a rubbery armband. The word is from the Latin *clitellae*, a packsaddle. Earthworms mate by lying next to each other, head to tail. Both secrete mucus until each is enclosed in a slime tube, after which they exchange sperm and eggs. Earthworms are essential to life, because they aerate the soil, enabling plants to grow   without

THE MODEL NOSE

'Hey, I thought you'd given up.'

'I have – these are for research.'

them, we'd all starve in short order. Cleopatra declared earthworms sacred: removing one from Egypt was an offence punishable by death. It's still legal to play the bassoon to them, however.

The nematode worm, *Caenorhabditis elegans* is one of the simplest of all animals and the probably the most thoroughly studied. It was the first animal to have its genome sequenced

It also likes nicotine and suffers terrible withdrawal symptoms once addicted

Tailpiece

The philosopher William James once wrote that a crab would be 'filled with a sense of personal outrage' if it could hear us class it as a crustacean. 'I am no such thing,' it would say. 'I am MYSELF, MYSELF alone.' With that in mind, we'd like to be able to declare that no animal has been intentionally insulted, misrepresented or traduced in the making of this book.

It is the product of much research by many people, and the only reason we haven't listed this is aesthetic – it would make it look and feel like a very different kind of book. If you would like information on our sources, or to correct or add to the information we have gathered, we would love to hear from you at www.qi.com/animalignorance

All mistakes are our own; all the best information has come from real scientists like Dr Joseph Garner at Purdue Unviersity, or the indefatigable efforts of the QI Elves. Special mention must go to Piers Fletcher, Justin Pollard, Garrick Alder, Xander Cansell, Vitali Vitaliev and to the regular members of the QI Talkboard who operate like an intellectual SWAT team, always on hand with original research and wise advice. Particular thanks are due to suze and dr. bob.

We'd also like to thank Stephen Page, Julian Loose, David

Watkins and the team at Faber for their faith and patience; Paula Turner for her keen editorial eye and linguistic sure-footedness; and Sarah Chaloner, Beatrice Gray, and Lorraine Heggessy at Talkback ThamesTV: this isn't much of a TV tie-in, but they helped make the space in which it was written.

Finally, thanks to Rachael, Sarah and Helen who have listened, advised, foraged, nurtured, and generally kept the kinship groups going while we hunted.

All the thoughts of a turtle
are turtle.
RALPH WALDO EMERSON

Index

Page numbers in *italics* denote an illustration